A Celebration of Friendship

A Celebration *of* Friendship

Melinda Rathjen, Editor

Guideposts

Published by Ideals Publications
A Guideposts Company
535 Metroplex Drive, Suite 250
Nashville, Tennessee 37211
www.idealsbooks.com

Color separations by Precision Color Graphics, Franklin, Wisconsin

Printed and bound in the United States of America

Publisher, Peggy Schaefer
Editor, Melinda Rathjen
Copy Editor, Kaye Dacus
Permissions Editor, Patsy Jay

Book designed by Marisa Jackson

1 3 5 7 9 10 8 6 4 2

All songs arranged by Dick Torrans

Cover: *La Cueillette* by Claude Fossoux. Image from Spiral Licensing.

Title page: *Summer Reflections* by Alexander Tiotrine. Image from Fine Art Photographic Library Ltd./
Walker Gallery Harrogate/Art Gallery Gerard, Wassenaar, Holland.

Additional Art Credits: Pages 6–7, *Les Enfants et les Cygnes* by Claude Fossoux; pages 32–33, *Dans les Graminés* by Claude Fossoux;
pages 56–57, *Jeune Fille en Rose* by Claude Fossoux; pages 70–71, *Promenade Dans les Champs* by Claude Fossoux;
pages 100–101, *La Cueillette* by Claude Fossoux; pages 126–127, *Le Champs de Coquelicots* by Claude Fossoux.
Images from Spiral Licensing. Background pattern throughout copyright © iStockphoto.com/Brendon De Suza.
Vector illustrations throughout copyright © iStockphoto.com/Jess Scholz.

ACKNOWLEDGMENTS

All Scripture quotations, unless otherwise noted, are taken from *The King James Version of the Bible.* Scripture quotations marked (NIV) are taken from the *Holy Bible, New International Version. Niv.* Copyright © 1973, 1978, 1984 by International Bible Society. Used by permission of Zondervan Publishing House. All rights reserved.
BURT BACHRACH for music and CAROL BAYER SAGER for words to "That's What Friends Are For." Copyright © 1982 by WB Music Corp., New Hidden Valley Music (rights administered by WB Music Corp). Warner-Tamerlane Publishing Corp. and Carole Bayer Sager Music (rights administered by Warner-Tamerlane Publishing Corp). All rights reserved. Used by permission of Alfred Publishing Co., Inc. BELLOW, SAUL. "On John Cheever." First published in *The New York Review of Books 2007.* Copyright © 2007 by Saul Below. Used by permission of the Wylie Agency. DIAMANT, ANITA. "Side by Side" from *Pitching My Tent.* Copyright © 2003 by author Anita Diamant. Published by Scribner, Simon & Schuster. DICKINSON, EMILY. "One Sister Have I in Our House." Reprinted by permission of the publishers and Trustees of Amherst College from *The Poems of Emily Dickinson: Variorum Edition.,* Ralph W. Franklin, ed., Cambridge Mass.: the Belknap Press of Harvard University Press © 1951, 1955, 1979, 1983 by the President and Fellows of Harvard College. DORNACHER, KARLA. "Grief Like a Shawl" from *The Blessing Of Friendship.* Copyright © 2000 by author Karla Dornacher. Published by J. Countryman imprint of Thomas Nelson. ELLEN GOODMAN and PATRICIA O'BRIEN. Excerpts from *I Know Just What You Mean.* Copyright © 2000 by the authors. Published by the Fireside imprint of Simon & Schuster. LARRY HENLEY and JEFF SILBAR for words and music to "The Wind Beneath My Wings." Copyright © 1982 Warner House of Music and WB Gold Music Corp. All Rights Reserved. Used by permission of Alfred Publishing Co., Inc. HOLMES, MARJORIE. "Friends Are Like Bracelet Charms" from *Love And Laughter,* by Marjorie Holmes. © 1959, 1967 by Marjorie Holmes Mighell. Used by permission of Dystel & Goderich Literary Management. JACKSON, SUZAN L. "The Start of a Beautiful Friendship" from *A Cup of Comfort For Friends,* edited by Colleen Sell. Published by Adams Media Corp. KEPHART, BETH. "Friends" and "Choosing Friends," excerpts from *Into The Tangle Of Friendship.* Copyright © 2000 by author Beth Kephart. Reprinted by permis-

sion of Houghton Mifflin Co. KIDDER, VIRELLE. "The Love Squad." Copyright © by Virelle Kidder. Previously published in *Decision* magazine, October 1999 by the Billy Graham Evangelistic Assoc. and in *Stories For A Kindred Heart,* by Multnomah Publishers, 2000. LEWIS, C. S. "On Friendship" from *C. S. Lewis Readings For Meditation And Reflection,* ed. by Walter Hooper. Copyright © 1992 by C. S. Lewis Pte Ltd. Published by HarperSanFrancisco. MOON, VICTORIA AUSTEN. "My Very Best Friend in the Whole Wide World" from *A Cup of Comfort for Friends* ed. by Colleen Sell, Published by Adams Media Corp., 2002. O'FAOLAIN, SEAN. "The Beginning of Friendship" from *Bird Alone* by Sean O'Faolain. Copyright © 1936 by Viking Press. ROGERS, FRED. Excerpt from *Life's Journeys According To Mister Rogers,* Copyright © 2005 by Family Communications, Inc. Published by Hyperion. SHAW, LUCI. "The Table As Icon" from *Friends for the Journey* by Madeleine L'Engle and Lucy Shaw. © 1997 by the authors. Regent College Publishing. TABER, GLADYS. "Portrait of a Friendship" from *Stillmeadow Calendar.* Copyright © 1967 by Gladys Taber, renewed © 1995 by Constance Taber Colby. Used by permission of Brandt and Hochman Literary Agents, Inc. TOTH, SUSAN ALLEN. An excerpt from *Blooming: A Small-Town Girlhood* by Susan Allen Toth, © 1981. Published by Little, Brown and Co. WELLS, JANE. "My Heart Still Grins" from *Woven on the Wind,* edited by Linda Hasselstrom, Gaydell Collier, and Nancy Curtis. © 2001 by the editors. Published by Houghton Mifflin Co. WOHLMUTH, SHARON J. "Photographs" from *Best Friends* by Sharon J. Wohlmuth and Carol Saline. Text © 1998 by Carol Saline. Published by Doubleday, an imprint of Random House.

Our thanks to the following authors or their heirs, some of whom we were unable to locate: George Matthew Adams, Laura L. Atkins, Anne Campbell Stark, Sandy Cayman, Thomas Curtis Clark, Wilma Echols, Hilda Butler Farr, Ruth B. Field, Thomas Hughes, Pamela Kennedy, Mary E. Linton, Linda MacFarlane, Helen Colwell Oakley, Mary O'Connor, Marilyn Romriell, Adeline Roseberg, Flora C. Rosenberg, Patricia La Rue Sanders, Harriet May Savitz, Harry Halsey Starrett, Estelle Taylor, and Flavia Weedn.

Every effort has been made to establish ownership and use of each selection in this book. If contacted, the publisher will be pleased to rectify any inadvertent errors or omissions in subsequent editions.

TABLE OF CONTENTS

THE MAKING OF FRIENDS

From quiet homes and first beginning,
Out to the undiscovered ends,
There's nothing worth the wear of winning
But laughter and the love of friends.
—HILAIRE BELLOC

A CELEBRATION OF FRIENDSHIP

*Blessed are they who have the gift of making friends,
for it is one of God's best gifts. It involves many things,
but above all, the power of going out of oneself and
appreciating whatever is noble and loving in another.*
—THOMAS HUGHES

THE BEGINNING OF FRIENDSHIP

Séan O'Faoláin

It was friendship in its first stage when one is giving all, spreading out all one's little riches, not yet having discovered either how much it is vain to offer or expect. That, I—who have for years tried to live alone—knew now, is how people do meet and join: a first slight bridge, a wavering feeler out of the shell of self; then a gush of willingness, giving with both hands; then, when all is given, the secret measuring by each of what—not of what the other has given but of what each has taken. The end and measure of utter friendship, the only release from the cave of loneliness, is with him who knows how to accept most. That discovery has meant everything to me. For as it is with men, so it is with life which we understand and love in proportion as we accept without question what it gives, without question as to whether we need it, nor even questioning whether its gift seems cruel or kind. It is the supreme generosity because we do not even know who the Giver is, why he has given, or what.

An Ocean of Devotion by Kathy Fincher   THE MAKING OF FRIENDS

My son was . . . cementing a friendship with special memories of times spent together, which could last a lifetime.

THE START OF A BEAUTIFUL FRIENDSHIP
Suzan L. Jackson

Can Michelle sleep over tonight? Pleeeease, Mom?" I must have sounded that familiar chant thousands of times while I was growing up.

My best friend, Michelle, and I loved sleepovers and spent countless nights at each other's house from the time we were about five years old until we left home for college in our late teens. Even after she moved to a town thirty miles away during our elementary school years, we remained close by spending weekends during the school year and entire weeks during the summer at one house or the other. Inseparable, we never seemed to tire of one another's company.

All of those wonderful memories of best friends and sleepovers came rushing back to me recently when my oldest son, Jamie, hosted his first overnight friend. Just a week earlier, he'd told me he wasn't quite ready to start sleepovers yet, and I'd assured him that he didn't have to until he felt comfortable. So imagine my surprise when a pleasant afternoon playing with his friend Danny ended with an until then unheard, but so familiar, refrain:

"Mommy, can Danny sleep over tonight? Please?"

The two boys looked at me expectantly, their faces glowing from having so much fun that they didn't want it to end. With memories of my own childhood sleepovers with Michelle dancing through my head, I tried to contain my enthusiasm while I quietly questioned Jamie whether he was really, really ready, given the discussion we'd had the week before.

His emphatic "Yes! Yes! Yes!" convinced me, and we asked Danny's mom. She said that Danny had gone on his first sleepover the previous week, and together we agreed the boys could sleep at our home that night, after a school picnic both families were attending. The boys' whoops of delight brought back to me that exhilarating feeling I'd felt at having my best friend with me for a whole night.

I think I was as excited as Jamie while we prepared for the picnic and planned the night ahead. My thoughts kept drifting back thirty years to my first sleepover with Michelle and to the many sleepovers that followed. We'd played games for hours, enjoyed special snacks, and, of course, stayed up late, talking and giggling.

Now, as The Mom, I was approaching sleepovers from an entirely new perspective, playing an important supporting role but no longer in the center of the excitement. It was my first time hosting a sleepover as a parent, and I wanted to start off on the right foot. My parents had always effortlessly embraced my friends within the circle of our family and made them feel at home. I wanted my sons' friends to feel as welcome and comfortable in our house as my friends had always been in my childhood home.

When we arrived at the school picnic, the boys greeted each other with big bear hugs, as if they hadn't seen each other in weeks. When it was time to leave, Danny's dad handed him his backpack and reminded us to call at any time if things didn't go well and Danny wanted to go home. He needn't have worried.

Despite the late hour, we let the boys have ice cream and watch a video when we got home. My husband and I kept saying to each other, "It's okay; this is a special night." Finally, it was bedtime.

We pulled out the trundle bed in Jamie's room and made it up. This alone was a thrilling event, the first time the trundle had been used, other than when his dad or I had slept in it when Jamie was sick. I read the boys a book, turned out the light, and said good night. I could tell Danny was feeling a little apprehensive at that point. I told the boys they could talk quietly for a while longer and left the room.

Immediately, I heard the door click softly behind me and saw the light go back on. I opened the door to see both boys sitting up with their Pokémon cards in their laps. Their faces, which just moments before had shown signs of unease, were now lit up with happiness. Remembering all those late nights with Michelle, I smiled and told them they could keep the light on a little longer. After staying up so late, I was sure they'd sleep in tomorrow.

At 7:30 the next morning, our two-year-old son,

Craig, ran into our room and woke me up with, "Where are Jamie and Danny?" The night before, he had been fascinated with the whole sleepover concept and couldn't believe that Jamie's friend was actually going to sleep at our house. I glanced at the clock as I forced myself awake and told him, "Shhhh. Jamie

Sailing Toy Boats by Edith Hume. Image from Fine Art Photographic Library Ltd./Courtesy of Bourne Gallery

and Danny are still sleeping in Jamie's room." Craig quickly replied, "No, they're not. I checked! Where are Jamie and Danny?"

I got up and tiptoed down the hall with him. Sure enough, the bed and trundle were already empty. Moments later, the older boys came running back up the stairs, already wide awake and laughing.

They had risen early and just picked up right where they'd left off the night before. I recalled then, through my early morning daze, that this was one of the greatest things about having a friend stay overnight. The fun didn't end until late at night, and then began again the moment you woke up in the morning, unencumbered by waiting for parents to get up or the delay of fun until morning routines were completed.

Their excitement continued all morning. They went from trading Pokémon cards to building with Legos to playing pirates to creating pictures together on the computer. Through it all, I heard not a single fight or harsh word between them. When it was time to take Danny home so that we could make it to a previous commitment on time, the boys pleaded, "Just a little longer? Please?"

Once again, I fell back in time and remembered Michelle and I spending days on end together, never tiring of each other's company. We'd play Monopoly or Clue for hours or spend an entire day pretending we were grownups and had an apartment together. Recording silly songs and pretend shows with our tape recorders could keep us busy for several days, as we ran around one house or the other, laughing together at our own private jokes.

The warmth and love of our special friendship has remained alive for over thirty years—through long-distance childhood moves, college, marriage, and children of our own. Now my son was embarking on the same kind of journey, cementing a friendship with special memories of times spent together, which could last a lifetime.

We took Danny home where the boys stood with their arms around each other, grinning like crazy, as I filled in Danny's mom on the highlights of the sleepover. After twenty-four hours spent almost constantly together, they both seemed exhilarated and euphoric, if a little tired. We left with promises of another sleepover, next time at Danny's house. I watched my normally hesitant son agree wholeheartedly to stay at his friend's house sometime soon. As we pulled out of the driveway, I smiled to myself and decided to write to Michelle when I got home. I might even suggest a Mommy sleepover.

Best Friends by Hans Andersen Brendekilde.
Image from Fine Art Photographic Library, London/ Art Resource, NY

CHOOSING FRIENDS

Beth Kephart

I am taken back to years ago when I chose my friends, then they chose me. Friendship, from the very start, was both exotic and pragmatic, a roughing up and a letting down. It was the way I shared what I loved and discovered what was worth sharing; the way I wasted the day, or fractions of day; the way I knew how big or strong or good or protected or likeable I—for that small instant—was. Friendship happened in neighborhoods and classrooms, and lasted for seconds and years. It turned trees into castles and marbles into coins, the streamers on a tricycle into wings of plastic glory.

THE SEEDS OF FRIENDSHIP

Marilyn Romriell

The seeds that start a friendship are kindness and a sweet smile. When you have a friendship started, you must give it nourishment, avoid the evils of jealousy and gossip that will stunt its growth, and learn to look for the good in others. Friendship thrives on love, trust, honesty, and understanding. Memories of experience shared with a friend will live on long after the friend is gone and will bring much joy to you. Friendship is a beautiful thing . . . cherish it.

There's something about childhood friends that you just can't replace.

—LISA WHELCHEL

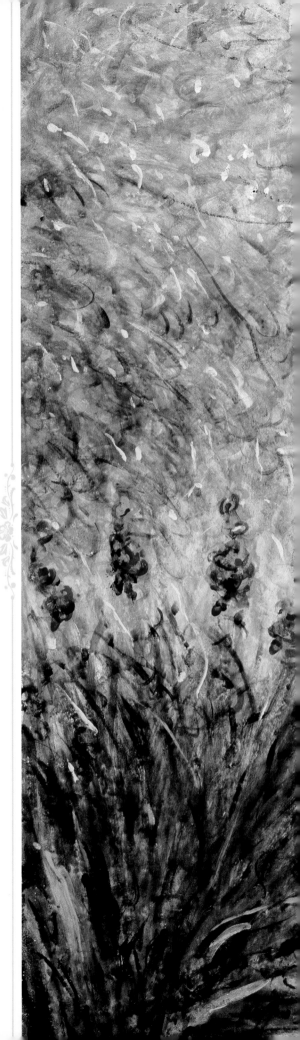

Concours de Bouquets by Claude Fossoux.
Image from Spiral Licensing

The More We Get Together

GERMAN FOLK MELODY

The more we get to- geth- er, to-

geth - er, to - geth - er, The

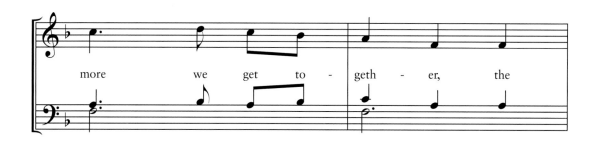

more we get to- geth - er, the

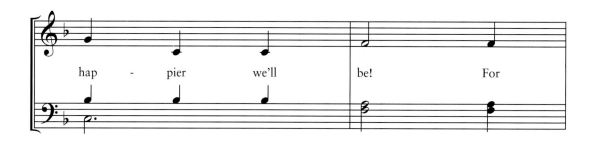

hap - pier we'll be! For

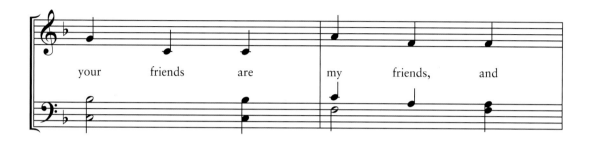

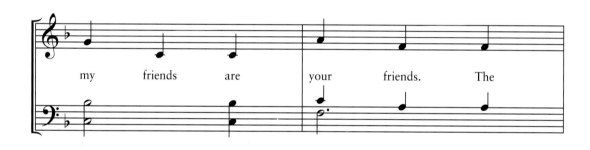

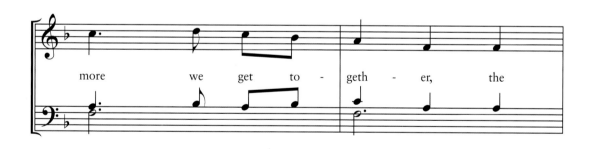

Hey! We could change our lives forever.
We could make ourselves into friends.

SIDE BY SIDE

Anita Diamant

I learned to spell the word *friend* in second grade. To help us master the pesky *i-e* combination, my teacher supplied a mnemonic device that still works for me: *Fri*day is the *end* of the week, which is when you see your *friends.*

Of course, in second grade I didn't have to wait until Saturday or Sunday. My best friend lived two doors down the block on Lehigh Avenue, so we saw each other every day. I have few clear memories of life before Ellen. We rode tricycles together before graduating to two-wheelers. We pretended glamorous adventures and domestic bliss with our dolls. We listened while our mothers told each other the gruesome tales of our births. We never had to *make* friends because we always knew everything there was to know about each other.

Friendship has never been quite that simple since, as I learned when my family moved to Denver and I walked through the doors of a junior high school where I was the only girl with pierced ears. After a long year of damp pillows, I was invited to a slumber party where I became part of a small circle who soon knew everything there was to know about me, from my loafers to my headbands, all the way through high school.

It wasn't hard keeping up with Becky and Jane and Sharon. We were in one another's classes by day and on the phone at night. We spent weekend afternoons on one another's couches, where we listened to the Beatles and Joni Mitchell and talked about boys, our parents, and—mostly—ourselves.

I recall thinking in college that I could lay the foundation of a solid friendship in the course of a single evening, between dinner and midnight. That's how long it took not only to tell the unexpurgated story of my life but also to listen to the entire history of an undergraduate peer. I spent many evenings like that and always woke up the next morning feeling right with the world.

Within a decade of graduation, everyone I knew was sighing about how hard it was to make a new friend, even if you worked side by side, even if you lived next door. Coworkers and neighbors almost never get the full story. We piece together bits of family lore, scraps from old love affairs, hints of sibling animosities—tidbits shaken loose during conversations about something else entirely.

When your children are young, it's especially hard to start the process. The frustration of *conversation interruptus* can unravel the thread of the most intimate exchange. Even if you're meeting in the relative peace of a kid-free workday lunch, the clock is always ticking.

It's an interesting locution—*making* friends. It reminds me of a greeting card with a lady in an apron whose bubble says, "For your birthday, I'm going to make you a cake . . . Poof! You're a cake." As if you could just run up to a likely candidate and shout, "Abracadabra! You're a friend."

To make friends, you need to mosey, to digress. In fact, you need a minimum of twenty-four uninterrupted, non-working hours. That's how long it takes to tell someone where you come from, what television shows you make a point of watching, and how you'd spend a million dollars. It's also important to share three meals and see each other's face by the light of morning, noon, and night.

I timed it. Valerie, a work acquaintance who lives in Manhattan, and I decided we wanted to become friends; so we booked a room in a country inn. I arrived around four; we started talking and didn't stop until long after the town's church clock filled our room with midnight bells.

The next morning we continued, comparing income, theology, cosmetics. We talked about our other friends and how we met our husbands. We admired each other's earrings. We compared photographs of our children. We talked about our travels and our health. We talked about the homeless and how we react when someone asks us for money on the street. We talked about living wills. We talked about movies

and movie stars and mothers. The experience was a little like going to summer camp, or a weekend at college. It was also a little sad, since we live miles apart. But our twenty-four hours sealed the deal between us.

Once you get past second grade, making friends requires a lot of effort. It's worth it. The

When You Get Big Like Me by Kathy Fincher

process bears some comparison with falling in love: there has to be a kind of mutual attraction. A signal is passed—some shared hilarity or a sentence finished with precisely the same words—and suddenly the room seems brighter. Hey! We could change our lives forever. We could make ourselves into friends.

THE EXTRAORDINARY INSTINCT

Arthur Christopher Benson

It is a mistake to think that one makes a friend because of his or her qualities; it has nothing to do with qualities at all. It is the person that we want, not what he does or says, or does not do or say, but what he is! That is eternally enough. Who shall explain the extraordinary instinct that tells us, perhaps after a single meeting, that this or that particular person in some mysterious way matters to us? I confess that, for myself, I never enter a new company without the hope that I may discover a friend, perhaps the friend, sitting there with an expectant smile. That hope survives a thousand disappointments. People who deal with life generously and large heartedly go on multiplying relationships to the end.

THE UNSPOKEN

Mark Rutherford

As a rule, we are unconscious of that which makes us precious to our friends. X, I am sure, has not the least notion why I love him. I doubt if he knows that he possesses what makes me love him.

We are friends, not through anything peculiar to us, but through the universal, the origin and property of us all.

For what do my friends stand? Not for the clever things they say: I do not remember them half an hour after they are spoken. It is always the unspoken, the unconscious, which is their reality to me.

Summertime by Mary Cassatt. Image from SuperStock

INTRODUCTIONS

Warm Spinach Dip

2 tablespoons butter

2 tablespoons olive oil

1¾ cups chopped onion

6 large garlic cloves, minced

2 tablespoons all-purpose flour

½ cup chicken stock or canned low-salt chicken broth

½ cup whipping cream

1 10-ounce package fresh spinach leaves

1 cup (packed) grated Parmesan cheese

¼ cup sour cream

½ teaspoon cayenne pepper

Baguette slices, toasted

MELT BUTTER WITH OIL in heavy large pot over medium heat. Add onion and garlic; sauté until onion is tender, about 6 minutes. Add flour; stir 2 minutes. Gradually whisk in stock and cream; bring to boil, whisking constantly. Cook until mixture thickens, stirring frequently, about 2 minutes. Remove from heat. Stir in spinach, cheese, sour cream, and cayenne (spinach will wilt). Season with salt and pepper. Transfer dip to serving bowl. Serve warm with toasted baguette slices. Makes 12 servings.

Baked Tortilla Chips

1 12-ounce package corn tortillas

1 tablespoon vegetable oil

3 tablespoons lime juice

1 teaspoon ground cumin

1 teaspoon chili powder

1 teaspoon salt

PREHEAT OVEN TO 350°F. Cut each tortilla into 8 chip-sized wedges and arrange the wedges in a single layer on a cookie sheet. In a spray bottle, combine the oil and lime juice. Mix well and spray each tortilla wedge until slightly moist. Combine the cumin, chili powder, and salt in a small bowl and sprinkle on the chips. Bake about 7 minutes. Rotate the pan and bake another 8 minutes or until the chips are crisp, but not too brown. Serve with salsas, garnishes, or guacamole. Makes 6 servings.

A great gathering can be kick-started with these delicious hors d'oeuvres. Invite new friends and old friends to share a snack, or begin a meal, with these starters.

Mushroom Balls

1	8-ounce package cream cheese			Butter
½	cup butter or margarine			Salt, black pepper, and
1	cup all-purpose flour			garlic powder to taste
	Pinch of salt		1	egg, beaten
1	pound fresh mushroom caps, washed and dried			

CREAM TOGETHER CHEESE AND BUTTER until well blended. Add flour and salt; mix well to form a dough. Chill 1 hour. Preheat oven to 425°F. Sauté mushroom buttons, rounded sides down first, in small amount of hot butter. Turn over and brown second side. Total cooking time should not exceed 2 to 3 minutes. Season with salt, pepper, and garlic powder. Let cool. Roll out dough to 9 x 12 inches and cut into 3-inch squares. Place mushrooms on each piece of dough and enclose, pinching ends, and rolling gently to form a ball. Place balls on lightly greased baking sheet and brush with beaten egg. Bake 20 minutes or until golden brown. Makes about 24 balls.

Crab Meat Dip

1	8-ounce package cream cheese, softened	½	teaspoon Worcestershire sauce
⅛	teaspoon salt	¾	cup sour cream or sour half-and-half
2	teaspoons lemon juice	1	tablespoon grated or minced onion
		2	6.5-ounce cans crab meat, minced

IN A LARGE BOWL, combine cream cheese, salt, lemon juice, Worcestershire sauce, and sour cream. Mix until smooth. Fold in onion and crab meat. Cover and chill at least 2 hours before serving. Makes 2 cups.

ON FRIENDSHIP

C. S. Lewis

Friendship arises out of mere companionship when two or more companions discover that they have in common some insight or interest or even taste in which the others do not share and which, till that moment, each believed to be his own unique treasure (or burden). The typical expression of opening friendship would be something like, "What? You too? I thought I was the only one." . . . It is when two such persons discover one another, when, whether with immense difficulties and semi-articulate fumblings or with what would seem to us amazing and elliptical speed, they share their vision—it is then that friendship is born. . . .

The shared activity and therefore the companionship on which friendship supervenes will not often be a bodily one like hunting or fighting. It may be a common religion, common studies, a common profession, even a common recreation. All who share it will be our companions; but one or two or three who share something more will be our friends. In this kind of love, as Emerson said, "Do you love me?" means "Do you see the same truth?"—or at least, "Do you care about the same truth?" The man who agrees with us that some question, little regarded by others, is of great importance, can be our friend. He need not agree with us about the answer.

We cannot tell the precise moment when friendship is formed. As in filling a vessel drop by drop, there is at last a drop which makes it run over; so in a series of kindnesses there is at last one which makes the heart run over.

—JAMES BOSWELL

Morning Light on the Terrace by Piotr Stolerenko.
Image From Fine Art Photographic Library Ltd./ Bourne Gallery,
Reigate/Art Gallery Gerard, Wassenaar, Holland

FRIENDS

Beth Kephart

Throughout our lives, friends enclose us, like pairs of parentheses. They shift our boundaries, crater our terrain. They fume through the cracks of our tentative houses, and parts of them always remain. They are the antidote not to our aloneness but to our loneliness. I think of someone sliding over on a bench. A chair being added to a circle. A letter sent for no good reason. A joke only two people understand. I think of the way an oak's roots hunger after water, suck life into the tree, anchor the pith, the heartwood, the windshake, the phloem, and keep the branches in their leaves. I think of someone looking up and saying, "Hey, I'm glad to see you." Someone indulging in the mathematics of plurals and finding more than expected in the sum. Friendship asks and wants, hollows and fills, ages with us and we through it, cradles us, finally, like family. It is ecology and mystery and language, all three. Fantastic, sustaining, bewildering, it requires us to explore and respect its multiplicity of forms and to teach our children its many lessons. To visit playgrounds where it all begins and wait and watch and remember.

*Great friendship is a delight . . .
a hyphen between two minds; a bridge
between two wills; a selfless joy in the
loving, giving, sharing, daring life;
where two outgivings merge into one,
two people lose their small "I" and
find new interest in a large "You."*
—ELIZABETH SELDEN

Keepers by Kathy Fincher

Be courteous to all but intimate with few;
and let those few be well tried before you give them
your confidence. True friendship is a plant of slow growth
and must undergo and withstand the shocks of adversity
before it is entitled to the appellation.
—GEORGE WASHINGTON

GOD GAVE THEM TO ME

Ralph Waldo Emerson

I awoke this morning with devout thanksgiving for my friends, the old and the new. Shall I not call God the beautiful, who daily showeth himself so to me in his gifts? I chide society, I embrace solitude, and yet I am not so ungrateful as not to see the wise, the lovely, and the noble minded, as from time to time they pass my gate. Who hears me, who understands me, becomes mine—a possession for all time. Nor is nature so poor but she gives me this joy several times, and thus we weave social threads of our own, a new web of relations; and, as many thoughts in succession substantiate themselves, we shall, by and by, stand in a new world of our own creation, and no longer strangers and pilgrims in a traditionary globe. My friends have come to me unsought. The great God gave them to me.

*Even before I met her in person, I knew I was going
to like Mary, for her friendly personality, cheerful voice,
and jolly laughter fairly lit up the line.*

MARY WAS HER NAME

Helen Oakley

Friendships are treasured rewards of life, especially for country folks. Country homes and farms are often isolated from the nearest neighbor and many miles from a town. When I was a little girl, it was delightfully exciting when one of my parents' friends was going to call on us. Amidst a flurry of activity, our house would be readied for company, and a full-course dinner would be prepared. My family, with even the kids spic-and-span, would gather by the door to welcome the visitor. I was impressed by the warm welcome our guest received, and learned at an early age that friends are special and friendships are to be valued.

When I was a young bride of nineteen, my husband and I settled on a farm in Pennsylvania. I was happy most of the time, but there were times when I was sad and very lonely. Everyone I knew was back in New York State; I missed my large family and all the relatives, neighbors, and friends so much that I was positive that I could never be content without them close by.

"You're sure to meet new friends," my mother would soothe, as I told her how lonely it was so far from home. Mom's prediction soon came true! Before

long, I became acquainted with a very friendly lady on the telephone party line who was known to everyone in Locust Hill as "Mary." There were twenty families on our party line, and it was one big, happy family with everyone acquainted with one another. Sometimes there would be several people conversing on the line, as one after the other would join in the conversation. How well I remember chatting with Mary, then suddenly hearing someone say, "That you, Mary?" And we would soon have a three-way conversation going.

Even before I met her in person, I knew I was going to like Mary, for her friendly personality, cheerful voice, and jolly laughter fairly lit up the party line. "How very much like Mom," I concluded one day as I hung up the receiver after chattering away with Mary just as though she were my own mother. Mary was great therapy for our countryside. I remember her best as someone to call on in time of need. When my babies were not feeling well, Mary's instructions over the phone soon had mother and babies feeling better.

Mary's large, white, homey farmhouse was up a picturesque, winding country lane at the foot of

Locust Hill mountain. Our farmhouse was several miles from Mary's home on the next mountain. She had more than enough to keep her busy on her own farm, but she always found time for others. If we did not have a sitter when we were going square-dancing at the grange hall, Mary would call over the party line and say, "Bring the kids on over; we'll get along just fine!" And they did, with Mary fussing over them just like they were her very own grandchildren. When we arrived to pick up the youngsters after midnight, Mary would have one on each knee, visiting merrily away as they all rocked to and fro in a large, comfortable rocking chair in the parlor. Close by, our baby snoozed in an old-fashioned cradle that had been brought out for the occasion.

Mary was also known far and wide for her cooking, especially her cartwheel sugar cookies. In all the years that I knew her, I never knew her to be out of those temptingly delicious cookies. Somehow, she always managed to have some in reserve for everyone who visited her farm, especially the children, who all seemed to have a special place in her heart. Seldom would Mary forget to ask the children, "Would you like to have some sugar cookies?" There was one time when she did forget to ask my children, and they finally asked her if she was going to ask them to have some sugar cookies, much to my embarrassment. Mary chuckled merrily as she hurried into the pantry, soon to reappear with a tray of cookies and a pitcher of fresh milk.

As a bride and later as a young mother miles away from family and friends, my problems would

often seem insurmountable, but then I would think of Mary, who was just a party line away. Talking things over with her on the line soon brightened up my little world. I was not lonely again, for I had

Sur la Terrasse by Max Nonnenbruch. Image from Fine Art Photographic Library Ltd./Haynes Fine Art

found a friend. She and I remained friends for many years on Locust Hill, then continued to be fast friends even after my husband and I moved away. I'm convinced the "Marys" of the world are few and far between; perhaps this is why they are so special!

MOMENTS WITH FRIENDS

Go oft to the house of thy friend,
for weeds choke the unused path.
—RALPH WALDO EMERSON

BLOOMING: A SMALL-TOWN GIRLHOOD

Susan Allen Toth

My girlfriends filled my days with the steady pulse of constant companionship. When I remember what I actually did, outside of school and evenings at home, I always see myself with one or more girlfriends.

What did we do? Mostly, I think, we talked. We talked on the buses, in the halls, at our lockers, in the classrooms, between classes in the restrooms, after school at the bus stop. Once home, we called each other up almost instantly and talked on the phone until some parent couldn't stand it any longer. Then we hung up for a while with promises to call back later. What on earth, our parents asked us, did we find to talk about? But it wasn't so much the topics we found engrossing, I think: the boys, teachers, clothes, gossip. All that talking built up a steady confidence that the trivia of our lives was worth discussion, that our *lives* were worth discussing, that we as individuals were worth someone's attention. "Do you think I ought to get my hair cut?" was a question that asked not only "How would I look with my hair shorter?" but "Do you *care* how I look?" Teachers snapped and lectured; parents discussed and argued; boys teased and muttered; but the steady hum of girlfriends, punctuated by laughter and whispers, was a reassuring continuo.

Besides talking, girlfriends went places with each other. No self-respecting boy would ever be seen shopping with a girl. We girls usually shopped in twos or threes, after school or on Saturday afternoons, not only to approve new purchases, but for the sheer fun of trying on new clothes. We were all known in Younkers; and although Mrs. Corter, the no-nonsense saleswoman, would tell us firmly to leave if someone else wanted the dressing room, until she did we could use the store as though it were a costume shop and we were actresses trying on different roles. Some afternoons we slipped into formals, very carefully, while Mrs. Corter hovered disapprovingly nearby, eagle-eyed for any rip or tear. We floated before the mirrors in layers of pink tulle or swooshes of yellow satin, admiring how much older we looked with bare shoulders and bone-in, strapless bodices. We tried on the new cotton spring dresses as soon as they arrived in midwinter, assuring Mrs. Corter that we were already "looking for an Easter dress." She wasn't fooled and whipped the dresses back to the racks as fast as we slipped them off. We giggled to each other, crowded into the tiny dressing room together, knowing her irritation.

Drifting up and down Main Street, we had regular rounds. We'd browse quickly through Penney's and Ward's, if we were really killing time, and maybe pause at Marty's, a collegiate sportswear shop. We didn't feel right yet in the Shetland sweaters and matching pleated skirts that Marty's sold to Iowa State girls. But we stroked the cashmere, sorted through cocktail dresses, and tried to imagine ourselves older and shapelier. We would only "look in" at Carole's, not daring to stay too long under the snooty, hard stares of the two sales-women with pouffed, lacquered hair, bright lipstick, and shiny nails. Then we'd wander toward the library, stop at Edith's Gift Shoppe to see whose new wedding patterns of silver and china were on display, or maybe drink a Coke at the Rainbow Café before catching the bus home. And all the time we talked, talked, talked.

The Birthday by Paul Attfield. Courtesy of www.ddfa.com

A Celebration of Friendship

Friends

ADELINE ROSEBERG

We share these loves, my friend and I:
Bubbling brooks, a pink and blue sky,
Delicate mists, soft winds that sing,
Fragile snowflakes, violets in spring.
We share these loves, my friend and I:
Ruffled curtains, a latticed pie,

Flower-filled vases, cozy nooks,
An open fire, rows of books.
We share these loves, my friend and I:
Happy thoughts, aims that are high,
The warmth of friendship, pleasure in giving,
Faith in God, and real joy in living.

To My Friend

ANNE CAMPBELL

I have never been rich before,
But you have poured
Into my heart's high door
A golden hoard.

My wealth is the vision shared,
The sympathy,
The feast of the soul prepared
By you for me.

Together we wander through
The wooded ways.

Old beauties are green and new
Seen through your gaze.

I look for no greater prize
Than your soft voice.
The steadiness of your eyes
Is my heart's choice.

I have never been rich before;
But divine,
Your step on my sunlit floor,
And wealth is mine!

Conversation Pieces

Cucumber Sandwiches

1 large cucumber, peeled	1 teaspoon salt
1 8-ounce package cream cheese, softened	¼ cup snipped green onion stems or snipped chives
½ teaspoon garlic salt	30 rounds or fingers of white bread, buttered
½ teaspoon Worcestershire sauce	

CUT CUCUMBER IN HALF LENGTHWISE; remove seeds. Dice and drain in a strainer for at least 1 hour. In a medium bowl, mix cream cheese, garlic salt, Worcestershire sauce, and salt until well blended. Stir in drained cucumber and snipped onion. Spread on buttered bread rounds. Make open-faced or closed sandwiches. Refrigerate, covered with waxed paper and a damp cloth, until serving time. Makes about 2½ dozen.

Watermelon Popsicles

2½ cups seeded diced watermelon	1 tablespoon plus 2 teaspoons fresh lemon juice
½ cup fresh raspberries or frozen unsweetened, thawed	1 tablespoon light corn syrup
6 tablespoons granulated sugar	

COMBINE ALL INGREDIENTS IN BLENDER; puree until smooth. Strain into 2-cup glass measuring cup, pressing on solids to extract as much liquid as possible. Pour ¼ cup of puree into each Popsicle mold. Freeze overnight. (Can be prepared 1 week ahead. Keep frozen.) Makes about 8 popsicles.

Share these treats with good friends on a summer afternoon and let the conversation flow. May the food and drink be as refreshing as the company.

Tea Punch

1 12-ounce canister frozen orange juice concentrate	3 tablespoons instant tea mix
1 6-ounce canister frozen limeade concentrate	1 liter ginger ale
	Sugar to taste
4½ cups water	Orange slices

IN A LARGE PITCHER, combine juice concentrates, water, and ginger ale; mix well. Add sugar to taste. Pour into punch bowl and garnish with orange slices, if desired. Makes 12 to 18 servings.

Blueberry Coffee Cake

2⅓ cups all-purpose flour, divided	½ teaspoon salt
¾ cup unsalted butter, room temperature, divided	1 cup granulated sugar
1 cup flaked sweetened coconut	2 large eggs
½ cup (packed) golden brown sugar	1 cup milk
1 teaspoon ground cinnamon	1 12-ounce package frozen blueberries, unthawed,
2½ teaspoons baking powder	or 2½ cups fresh preparation

PREHEAT OVEN TO 375°F. In a medium bowl, combine ⅓ cup flour, ¼ cup butter, coconut, brown sugar, and cinnamon. Mix until moist and crumbly. Set aside. Sift remaining 2 cups flour, baking powder, and salt into small bowl. In a large bowl, beat remaining ½ cup butter until fluffy. Gradually add sugar, beating until well blended. Add eggs 1 at a time, beating to blend after each addition. Add dry ingredients alternately with milk approximately ⅓ at a time, mixing until well blended. Fold in blueberries. Transfer batter to greased and floured 13 x 9 x 2-inch baking pan. Sprinkle coconut mixture evenly over top. Bake about 40 minutes, or until tester inserted into center comes out clean and topping is golden brown. Cool cake slightly. Serve warm or at room temperature. Makes 12 servings.

*The time you enjoy wasting
is not wasted time.*
—BERTRAND RUSSELL

A Time to Talk
ROBERT FROST

When a friend calls to me from the road
And slows his horse to a meaning walk,
I don't stand still and look around
On all the hills I haven't hoed,
And shout from where I am, "What is it?"
No, not as there is a time to talk.
I thrust my hoe in the mellow ground,
Blade-end up and five feet tall,
And plod: I go up to the stone wall
For a friendly visit.

*Friends are there when
your hopes are raveled
and your nerves
are knotted; talking about
nothing in particular,
you can feel the tangles untwist.*
—PAM BROWN

Picking Flowers in an Alpine Meadow by Hans Dahl. Image from Fine Art
Photographic Library Ltd./Courtesy of Polak Gallery, London

THE VERY BEST THING

Henry van Dyke

The very best thing is good talk, and the thing that helps it most is friendship. How it dissolves the barriers that divide us and loosens all constraints and diffuses itself like some fine old cordial through all the veins of life—this feeling that we understand and trust each other and wish each other heartily well! Everything into which it really comes is good. It transforms letter writing from a task to a pleasure. It makes music a thousand times more sweet. The people who play and sing not *at* us but *to* us—how delightful it is to listen to them! Yes, there is a talkability that can express itself even without words. There is an exchange of thoughts and feeling which is happily alike in speech and in silence. It is quietness pervaded with friendship.

*How rare it is to be able
to get into that kind of conversation
with a friend that goes on
for years and years and just
continues underneath everything.*
—Marge Piercy

I've Gotta Secret by Kathy Fincher

We danced without moving, we sang without saying a word,
and we laughed out loud to be part of this night
and each other. It was a celebration.

MY HEART STILL GRINS

Jane Wells

It was the time of day when the sun hesitates to call it quits and ranchers feel honest if they've given their best and relieved if they haven't. The big barn doors were latched open, and horse traffic was calm and easy. I sat on the back of an old flatbed used for feeding, still warm from the sun, savoring an after-dinner cup of coffee. A friend who boarded her horse with us introduced me to her guest, another woman with a sincere smile and kind eyes. Offering them refreshment, I left for the house to pour a glass of iced tea, brew a cup of herbal tea, refill my coffee, and set out cookies baked that afternoon. It was important to me that our anticipated visit be as relaxing as my hospitality could provide. I hoped the barn cats would not try to sip our drinks and the dogs would not beg for cookies, but I never suggested we visit in the house.

The three of us found places to perch in front of the open barn doors. We wore matching outfits of sweat-stained jeans that were worn and faded, thin cotton shirts covered with horse hair, dusty boots, and hairstyles never featured in fashion magazines. Oh, we were a sight as we got comfortable on overturned feed buckets.

We talked of things that define us: a new colt, a sweet mare, where we came from, how we got here, hinting about lost loves and tears shed but long since dried on our pillows. There was bittersweet, but no bitterness.

All the while, the bright light faded into softer colors until our edges became subtle outlines. Still we talked, quieter now as the night sounds came and the animals settled down.

My friend, with her goofy sense of humor and delight in living, jumped up and announced the grand finale. She would play a song we just had to hear. Finding the tape in her Volkswagen with the back seat removed to make room for her dogs, she filled those empty spaces inside and those shadows outside with crazy music—a country song with a Cajun beat. Oh, it was just perfect: "Mad Cowboy Love."

We danced without moving, we sang without saying a word, and we laughed out loud to be part of this night and each other. It was a celebration. Three women, three friends, sharing the best of times; and I knew, without any doubt, that this night would count mightily toward reckoning the good and the bad.

Bench by Natalie Levine.
Image from Spiral Licensing

Moments with Friends

A man must get friends as he would get
food and drink for nourishment and sustenance.

THE EXCITEMENT OF FRIENDSHIP

Randolph Bourne

We have as many sides to our character as we have friends to show them to. Quite unconsciously I find myself witty with one friend, large and magnanimous with another, petulant and stingy with another, wise and grave with another, and utterly frivolous with another. I watch with surprise the sudden and startling changes in myself as I pass from the influence of one friend to the influence of someone else. But my character with each particular friend is constant. I find myself, whenever I meet him, with much the same emotional and mental tone. If we talk, there is with each one some definite subject upon which we always speak and which remains perennially fresh and new. If I am so unfortunate as to stray accidentally from one of these well-worn fields into another, I am instantly reminded of the fact by the strangeness and chill of the atmosphere. We are happy only on our familiar levels, but on these we feel that we could go on exhaustless forever, without a pang of ennui. And this inexhaustibility of talk is the truest evidence of good friendship.

Friends do not, on the other hand, always talk of what is nearest to them. Friendship requires that there be an open channel between friends, but it does not demand that that channel be the deepest in our nature. It may be of the shallowest kind and yet the friendship be of the truest. For all the different traits of our nature must get their airing through friends, the trivial as well as the significant. We let ourselves out piecemeal it seems, so that only with a host of varied friends can we express ourselves to the fullest. Each friend calls out some particular trait in us, and it requires the whole chorus fitly to teach us what we are. This is the imperative need of friendship. A man with few friends is only half developed; there are whole sides of his nature which are locked up and have never been expressed. He cannot unlock them himself, he cannot even discover them; friends alone can stimulate him and open them. Such a man is in prison; his soul is in penal solitude. A man must get friends as he would get food and drink for nourishment and sustenance. And he must keep them, as he would keep health and wealth, as the infallible safeguards against misery and poverty of spirit.

Silence Shared

MARY E. LINTON

Then come again and share this quietness . . .
Deeper the silence while you are away
And yet, a richer silence, I confess,
For those brief hours . . . winged moments of a day!
Come with your vision pushing back these walls
Till new horizons echo your deep voice,
Catching the distant note of one who calls
And listens for the answer of his choice.
Oh, come and share the music and the laughter,
The understanding words, the open book,
The coffee and the banter that comes after,
The memory of a long and wordless look.
Silence is golden; we shall not forsake it . . .
But silence is best when there are two to break it.

STILLNESS TOGETHER

Henri Nouwen

A friend is that other person with whom we can share our solitude, our silence, and our prayer. A friend is that other person with whom we can look at a tree and say, "Isn't that beautiful?"; or sit on the beach and silently watch the sun disappear under the horizon. With a friend we don't have to say or do something special. With a friend we can be still and know that God is there with both of us.

Kind Words Are Dear to All

Nelly E. Elwell

P. E. Van Noorden

Speak gen - tly, there's e-nough of care! Be - neath the bright-est smile, The lips may ut - ter mer - ry words, The heart be sad the while, The heart be sad the while. A kind word is a lit - tle thing, But

Friendship

DINAH MARIA MULOCK CRAIK

Oh, the comfort—the inexpressible comfort
of feeling safe with a person,
Having neither to weigh thoughts
Nor measure words—but pouring them
All right out—just as they are—
Chaff and grain together—
Certain that a faithful hand will
Take and sift them—
Keep what is worth keeping—
And, with the breath of kindness,
Blow the rest away.

A FRIEND

Author Unknown

What is a friend? I'll tell you. It is a person with whom you dare to be yourself. Your soul can go naked with him. He seems to ask you to put on nothing, only to be what you really are.

When you are with him, you do not have to be on your guard. You can say what you think, so long as it is genuinely you. He understands those contradictions in your nature that cause others to misjudge you.

With him you breathe freely—you can avow your little vanities and envies and absurdities; and, in opening them up to him, they are dissolved on the white ocean of his loyalty. He understands. You can weep with him, laugh with him, pray with him—through and underneath it all he sees, knows, and loves you.

A friend, I repeat, is one with whom you dare to be yourself.

MOMENTS WITH FRIENDS

With a friendship such as I have with Faith, there is a sharing of the essential self which makes one a better person, I think.

PORTRAIT OF A FRIENDSHIP

Gladys Taber

In midwinter, Faith Baldwin comes for a visit. We may not have seen each other since fall, but Faith blows in like a leaf (all eighty-five pounds of her), picking up conversation where we left off when we said goodbye. We talk right on through the day and far into the night, and I am glad no tape recorder is around because we sip from the world situation to the latest Bruce Catton book, from the new styles in clothes (we never like them) to what the children (her three and my one) have been doing.

Faith is a companion for good times but also for difficult ones, for her spirit is as valiant as her tongue is witty. The time the furnace went off in the night and it was ten degrees below zero, Jill and I were in a dither; but Faith appeared for breakfast in her fur coat and said probably someone would fix it in time. When the stove went off, she said sandwiches were fine and cold coffee was good for you. And when we have a flat tire, she comments on what a lovely day it is. Nothing disturbs her inner tranquility, and yet she is not what most people think of as a tranquil person: she is volatile and quick, with moods as variable as quicksilver itself.

She is equally at home at an elegant party or sitting in the kitchen eating milk toast. She loves mashed potatoes and gravy, fried tomatoes, salt pork in creamed sauce, and most of the less gourmet foods just as well as lobster soufflé or trout amandine.

When we discuss ourselves, as we do now and then, she says I am too outgoing; I just love everybody, but when I dislike someone it is lethal. I tell her she has a gift for analyzing everyone she sees, but she can be too critical. At that point we generally go back to our jigsaw puzzle and work in silence.

Friendship is a treasure that cannot be overrated. Sometimes as we dash through life, I think, we fail to consider that without the holding of friends (that is the only word for it) we should be in quicksand much of the time. The few people I know who take no pains to be friends are a stern and rock-bound sort and, I notice, seldom laugh. When I happen to see them, I feel a bridge of distance like the Golden Gate is between my shore and theirs.

With a friendship such as I have with Faith, there is a sharing of the essential self which makes one a better person, I think. We are closely attuned; often I say the first word of a sentence and she completes it; or, if we are out with a number of people, someone will make a remark, and by a flick of an eyelash we tell each other just what we think of that idea.

Yet some people are surprised at this since we are so different, as people keep pointing out, and have been for thirty years. They tell me I am a housewife at heart, a cook, a dog addict, a cat lover, a pushover for babies; whereas she doesn't know how to measure a cup of anything, is never involved with a vacuum cleaner, has no dog or cat, and never acts like an idiot at seeing a baby go by in a carriage. But I think a lifelong friendship is founded not on two people being alike but in a deeper sense of community spirit. Faith's compassion and inherent sensibility and devotion to large issues and generosity are basic, so why should I care whether she knows how to make a cheese soufflé or cope with burned-out light bulbs?

That old tired saying "No man is an island" is profoundly true. A sea of differences may stretch between two people, but it is possible to cross it if both are willing.

Japonica and Bluebells by Piotr Stolerenko. Image from Fine Art Photographic Library Ltd./ Bourne Gallery, Reigate/Art Gallery Gerard, Wassenaar, Holland

THE HEART GROWS FONDER

Nothing makes the earth seem so spacious
as to have friends at a distance;
they make the latitudes and longitudes.
—HENRY DAVID THOREAU

LONG-DISTANCE FRIENDS

Pamela Kennedy

I was browsing in a gift shop the other day, and a small wall hanging caught my eye. On a piece of rough board, the artist had painted a colorful garden. Small lavender violets clustered in front of a row of daisies. Behind these, roses and snapdragons bloomed. A line of sunflowers stood guard at the garden's border, and, in the distance, a sheltering barrier of evergreens filled the background. Arched over the top of the plaque were the words "Friendship Is Life's Garden."

This idea of friendship as a garden intrigued me. I mentally inventoried my friends, deciding which were sensitive violets, which were cheerful daisies, which were elegant roses, and which were practical and optimistic sunflowers. I must admit I even ventured to identify a few weeds in my musings! Then I recalled the row of trees standing in the background of the artist's scene. I'm not sure if these were meant to be included in friendship's garden, but for me they became a powerful image of a very special kind of friend I treasure: my long-distance friends.

Thirty years of marriage to a military man have offered many wonderful opportunities to make new friends and an equal number of occasions to leave them behind as we moved thousands of miles away to a new assignment. Some of my more stationary acquaintances doubt the possibility of maintaining friendships with people one doesn't see for years. I like to tell them distance isn't really a barrier to friendship, it only adds a new dimension to it.

Like the trees in the artist's picture, my long-distance friends offer a sense of perspective to my life. I can see them in memories that tower above the circumstances of today reminding me of times we shared joy, challenge, sadness, and triumph together. Just like the wind and rain and sun shape the development of a tree, my friends helped to shape me by their influence, example, and encouragement.

I met Nan when she was a patient in a hospital where I was doing volunteer work about twenty-five years ago. I felt so sorry for this beautiful mother of six because she suffered from constant pain and was confined to a wheelchair. With the thought of cheering her up, I visited her often, and we spent several hours sharing our thoughts on life and faith. I'm not sure if my immature attempts to offer solace accomplished much in her life, but her wit and wisdom made a profound difference in mine. She gently demonstrated that true joy and peace are more a matter of internal circumstances than external, that a deep and abiding confidence in God transcends our present doubts, and that family is the context in which we learn about love—both giving and receiving. Her words strengthened me like the nourishing rain strengthens the trunk of a tree, enabling it to grow until it is able to withstand a storm without being broken. I have seen Nan only a handful of times since we were first friends; but each time I feel tested by the winds of a storm, I recall her strength and am encouraged to endure with her grace.

Another friend, Terry, was with me twenty years ago when my second son was born. My husband was overseas, and Terry filled in as my labor and delivery coach. She and I shared an incredible experience and will always be joined by that bond of birth. When her army husband was transferred overseas, I grieved like I was losing a member of my family. Although we corresponded by mail, it was fifteen years before we met again; and, when that happened, we picked up as if we had only been apart for a few weeks! Our children had grown, our lives and circumstances had changed; but, like the towering evergreens, our roots are intertwined at a deep level, and we will always be together there. In a small Wisconsin town several years ago, Lynn and I raised toddlers together. We shared all the triumphs and trials of toilet training, tumbles, and temper tantrums. We debated the merits of breast and bottle, whole grain and processed, scheduling and spontaneity. At one time we saw each other several times a day, but now we are fortunate to visit once every few years. Our children are now young men and women, but our mutual experiences as new mothers still bind the

two of us together. Like the trees, we stand apart; but when the winds of chance and circumstance allow, our branches touch once more, and our lives intermingle again like the fragrant boughs.

In the garden of friendship, the colorful blossoms blooming the closest may get the lion's share of our attention, but I have learned to also treasure the

La Lettre by Abraham Solomon. Image from Fine Art Photographic Library Ltd./Walker Galleries

trees standing in the background. Just like that row of evergreens in the artist's painting, long-distance friends provide both perspective and beauty; the perspective of the past and the beauty of shared memories adding a depth of experience to our lives that only time and patience can produce.

CARE PACKAGES

Snickerdoodles

2¾ cup sifted all-purpose flour	1½ cups sugar
2 teaspoons cream of tartar	2 eggs
1 teaspoon baking soda	2 tablespoons granulated sugar
½ teaspoon salt	2 teaspoons cinnamon
1 cup shortening, softened	

IN A MEDIUM BOWL, sift together flour, cream of tartar, baking soda, and salt. In a large bowl, combine shortening, sugar, and eggs. Stir in flour mixture. Cover and chill at least 1 hour. Preheat oven to 400°F. In a small bowl, sift together sugar and cinnamon. Form dough into 1-inch balls and roll each in sugar mixture. Place 2 inches apart on an ungreased cookie sheet. Bake 8 to 10 minutes, or until lightly browned but still soft (cookies will flatten as they cool). Makes 5 dozen cookies.

Peanut Butter Cookies

1½ cups flour	½ cup brown sugar
½ teaspoon baking soda	½ cup peanut butter
½ teaspoon salt	1 egg
½ cup shortening	½ teaspoon vanilla
½ cup plus 2 tablespoons granulated sugar	

PREHEAT OVEN TO 350°F. In a small bowl, combine flour, baking soda, and salt. In a large bowl, combine shortening, ½ cup granulated sugar, and brown sugar. Add peanut butter, egg, and vanilla, mixing well. Stir flour mixture into peanut butter mixture until dough forms. Cover and chill until dough is easy to handle. Shape into 1-inch balls and flatten with fork dipped in remaining sugar. Bake 10 to 15 minutes. Makes 3 dozen cookies.

A gift of food can be an expression of love to friends, whether their skies are cloudy or blue. Share these treats with friends near and far.

Lemon Bars

1	14-ounce can sweetened condensed milk	1	cup brown sugar
½	cup lemon juice	½	teaspoon salt
1	teaspoon lemon extract	1	cup uncooked oatmeal
½	cup butter or margarine	1½	cup sifted flour
		1	teaspoon baking powder

PREHEAT OVEN TO 350°F. Mix together milk, lemon juice, and lemon extract; set aside. In a large bowl, cream butter and sugar; add remaining ingredients. Cover bottom of 9 x 9-inch baking pan with half of oatmeal mixture. Spread lemon filling evenly over top. Sprinkle remaining oatmeal mixture on top. Bake 25 minutes. Let cool before cutting. Makes 16 servings.

Hot Banana Bread

2	cups sifted all-purpose flour	2	eggs
1½	teaspoons baking powder	1	cup sugar
½	teaspoon baking soda	8	tablespoons melted butter
½	teaspoon salt	1½	tablespoons buttermilk
½	cup seedless raisins	1	teaspoon lemon juice
½	cup dried apricots	½	cup chopped walnuts
1	cup mashed banana		

PREHEAT OVEN TO 350°F. In a medium bowl, sift flour, baking powder, baking soda, and salt. Set aside. Rinse raisins and apricots under cold water and dry; mince coarsely. Combine raisins and apricots with walnuts. Sprinkle 2 tablespoons of flour mixture over fruit and nuts; toss to coat all pieces. Set aside. In a large bowl, combine banana, eggs, sugar, butter, buttermilk, and lemon juice; beat until smooth. Gradually add the remaining flour mixture; stir until well blended. Stir in the fruit and nut mixture. Pour into a greased and floured Bundt pan; bake 1 hour. Serve warm. Note: the flavor of the bread develops best if wrapped and left at room temperature 1 to 2 days. Can be frozen. To serve, wrap in aluminum foil and warm in a preheated 300°F oven about 15 minutes. Makes 12 to 16 servings.

Letters

RUTH B. FIELD

A few words drifting over time and space
Can bring a warmth, a glow of friendliness;
A voice unheard, a loved one's absent face
Return with written words. A soft caress,
The echo of an old forgotten song
Between the lines; a sudden, clear reflection
To fill the heart with pleasure, deep and strong,
Brings back again a voice's dear inflection.
Across the miles, the handclasp of a friend
Reaches out within a letter's lines;
And, down a little lane, dream footsteps wend
Where memory's flowered tendril greenly twines.
From homefolks come small messages we love:
Just little things that bring a bit of cheer;
And like sun smiling through clouds above
Are cherished words of someone we hold dear.
Oh, letters are like angels without wings
That come to us as if on magic flight,
Can evoke tears or happiness that sings—
Bright little flames that light the darkest night.

*Please never stop writing
me letters—they always
manage to make me feel
like my higher self.*
—ELIZABETH BISHOP

ON JOHN CHEEVER

Saul Bellow

ohn and I met at irregular intervals all over the U.S. I gave him lunch in Cambridge; he bought me a drink in Palo Alto. He came to Chicago; I went to New York. Our friendship, a sort of hydroponic plant, flourished in the air. It was, however, healthy, fed by good elements; and it was a true friendship. Because we met in transit, as it were, we lost no time in getting down to basics. On both sides there was instant candor. The speed at which necessary information was exchanged was wonderfully amusing. Each of us knew what the other was. We worked at the same trade which, in America, is a singularly odd and difficult one practiced by difficult people who are not always pleased by the talents of their contemporaries. John was not in the least grudging or rivalrous. Like the late John Berryman, he was fabulously generous with other writers. Yes, an odd lot, poets and writers of fiction; and to those who write novels about it, the country, too, is singularly paradoxical, very different from the "normal" America that businessmen, politicians, journalists and trade unionists, advertising men and scientists, engineers and farmers live in.

I think that the differences between John and me endeared us more to each other than the affinities. He was a Yankee; I, from Chicago, was the son of Jewish immigrants. His voice, his style, his humor were different from mine. His manner was reticent, mine was—something else. It fell to John to resolve these differences. He did this without the slightest difficulty, simply by putting human essences in first place: first the persons—himself, myself—and, after that, the other stuff, class origins, social history. A fairly experienced observer, I have never seen the thing done as he did it—done, I mean, as if it were not done at all but flowed directly from his nature.

Tea on the Terrace by Piotr Stolerenko. Image from Fine Art Photographic Library Ltd./ Bourne Gallery, Reigate/Art Gallery Gerard, Wassenaar, Holland

You can kiss your family and friends goodbye
and put miles between you; but, at the same time,
you carry them with you in your heart,
your mind, your stomach, because you do not
just live in a world but a world lives in you.

—FREDERICK BUECHNER

SEEDS

Rose Fay Thomas

The exchange of seeds and plants which always attends garden visits is one of the pleasant incidents connected with them. My garden is a veritable album; and, as I wander over our place, I find many a dear friend or happy hour commemorated in it. This little clump of oxalis, naturalized so prettily in the woods, was gathered one lovely day when a merry party joined us in an expedition to the Profile Notch. That group of lady's slippers came from the woods of a dear friend in Vermont. Here are moss roses from a magnificent rose garden in Massachusetts, and there are seedlings from the home of Longfellow, or willows rooted from cuttings brought from the South by Frederick Law Olmsted. Hardly a flower-loving friend have I who has not left an autograph in plant or shrub or tree in my garden, and, in like manner, many a thrifty plant has left my borders for those of distant friends.

Feeding the Doves by Ernest Walbourn.
Image from Fine Art Photographic Library
Ltd./Gavin Graham Gallery, London

THE HEART GROWS FONDER

A Perfect Day

CARRIE JACOBS-BOND

Well, this is the end of a per-fect day, Near the

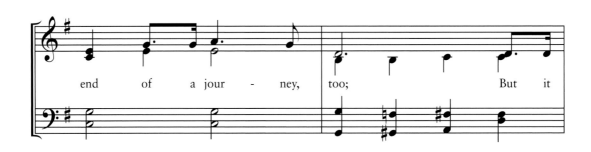

end of a jour-ney, too; But it

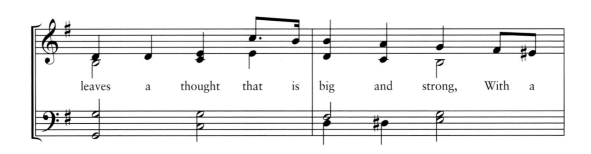

leaves a thought that is big and strong, With a

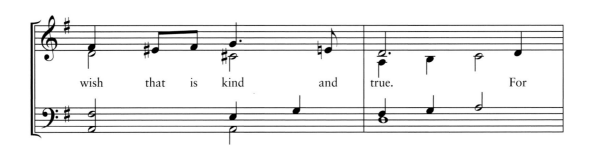

wish that is kind and true. For

mem - 'ry has paint - ed this per - fect day With

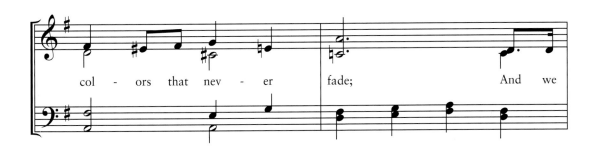

col - ors that nev - er fade; And we

find, at the end of a per - fect day, The____

soul of a friend we've made.

INSPIRING EACH OTHER

If, instead of a gem or even a flower, we should cast the gift of a loving thought into the heart of a friend, that would be giving as the angels give.
—GEORGE MACDONALD

*If you truly love and enjoy your friends,
they are a part of the golden circlet that makes life good.*

FRIENDS ARE LIKE BRACELET CHARMS

Marjorie Holmes

It was a party, in the truest sense of the word. An assortment of interesting people, small enough so that strangers could become acquainted, old friends could talk; yet large enough to be full of laughter and music and pleasantries and stimulating new contacts.

On impulse I remarked to our hostess, Peg Howe, "You certainly have a lot of lovely friends."

"Oh, yes," she laughed. And lifting her braceleted arm she remarked, "My friends are the charms on my bracelet of life."

The charms! I thought. Why—yes. The enhancements, the adornments—that extra shining something. If you truly love and enjoy your friends, they are a part of the golden circlet that makes life good.

When you gather them about you, you feel happy—and proud. Their accomplishments add a glow to your own being. What's more, you want to share them: "He's a distinguished surgeon, and his wife makes a home for all these foreign students—you must meet them." . . . "They both do little theater work, you'll just love them, they're both so alive—" . . . "He

plays folk songs on the guitar and sings in three languages—" . . . "Now that the children are in school she's studying law." . . .

But not only their accomplishments, their qualities: "Helen is the most generous person I've ever known." . . . "Grace has the most beautiful brown eyes—when she talks they just shine—" . . . "Jim has a laugh that makes you feel good all over. And you can depend on what he says, he'd never let you down—"

The person who can feel and speak this way about his friends is truly blessed. His life is rich in meaningful relationships. His friends are not a source of criticism and carping and jealousy and gossip. They are people truly dear to him, so dear that he can't refrain from singing their praises to others. And in so doing he is always making new ones. For the way a person feels about his friends is a pretty accurate indication of the kind of person he or she is.

The man or woman who treasures his friends is usually solid gold himself.

Friendship

CORINNE ROOSEVELT ROBINSON

Though love be deeper, friendship is more wide;
Like some high plateau stretching limitless,
It may not feel the ultimate caress
Of sun-kissed peaks, remote and glorified;
But here the light, with gentler winds allied,
The broad horizon sweeps till loneliness,
The cruel tyrant of the soul's distress,
In such sweet company may not abide.
Friendship has vision, though dear love be blind,
And swift and full communion in the fair,
A free flight of high and sudden ecstasy;
The broad excursions where, mind knit to mind,
And heart renewed, can all things dare,
Lit by the fire of perfect sympathy.

Pour Generously

MARY O'CONNOR

From the pitcher holding friendship,
One can pour and never find
That the pitcher ever empties;
Somehow it is magic-lined.
Every drop that leaves that pitcher
Leaves a larger drop behind.

Garden Table with Blue Chair by Piotr Stolerenko.
Image from Fine Art Photographic Library Ltd./Walker Gallery
Harrogate/Art Gallery Gerard, Wassenaar, Holland

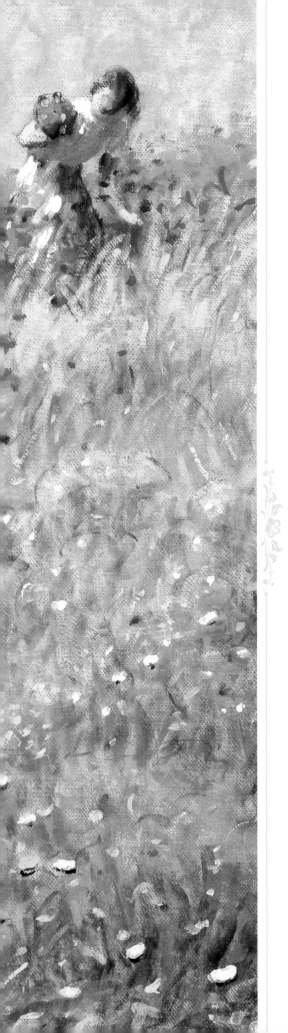

A friend may well be reckoned the masterpiece of nature.
—Ralph Waldo Emerson

True Nobility

Richard Wagner

My Dear Liszt:

I must say, you are a friend. Let me say no more to you, for although I always recognized in friendship between men the noblest and highest relation, it was you who embodied this idea into its fullest reality by letting me no longer imagine, but feel and grasp, what a friend is. I do not thank you, for you alone have the power to thank yourself by your joy in being what you are. It is noble to have a friend, but still nobler to be a friend.

So long as we love, we serve;
so long as we are loved by others,
I would almost say that
we are indispensable;
and no man is useless
while he has a friend.
—Robert Louis Stevenson

The Wind Beneath My Wings

LARRY HENLEY AND JEFF SILBAR

1. It must have been cold there in my shad - ow,
2. So I was the one with all the glo - ry,

to nev - er have the sun - light on your face.
while you were the one with all the strength.

You were con - tent to let me shine, that's your way;
A beau - ti - ful face with-out a name for so long,

you al-ways walked a step be - hind.
a beau - ti - ful smile to hide the pain.

Did you ev- er know that you're my he - ro,

and ev - ery-thing I would like to be?

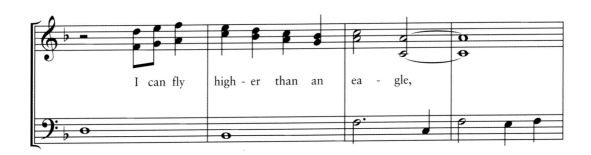

I can fly high - er than an ea - gle,

'cause you are the wind be - neath my wings.

WHILE SUCH FRIENDS ARE NEAR

Helen Keller

Those are red-letter days in our lives when we meet people who thrill us like a fine poem; people whose handshake is brimful of unspoken sympathy; and whose sweet, rich natures impart to our eager, impatient spirits a wonderful restfulness which, in its essence, is divine. The perplexities, irritations, and worries that have absorbed us pass like unpleasant dreams, and we wake to see with new eyes and hear with new ears the beauty and harmony of God's real world. The solemn nothings that fill our everyday life blossom suddenly into bright possibilities. In a word, while such friends are near us, we feel that all is well. Perhaps we never saw them before, and they may never cross our life's path again; but the influence of their calm, mellow natures is a libation poured upon our discontent, and we feel its healing touch, as the ocean feels the mountain stream freshening its brine.

ANOTHER VIEW

Ellen Goodman and Patricia O'Brien

A new friend can reintroduce a woman to herself, allowing her to look at herself with a new pair of eyes and a different mindset. The younger sister cast as "daffy" by the family is seen as "funny"—and fun—by a friend. The melodramatic wife is welcomed as a rich storyteller. More often than not, through close friendships, women see themselves through another lens, experience a new kind of self-consciousness. Flaws can be recast as strengths, self-doubts lifted by acceptance. Friends help define and motivate each other.

Carnation, Lily, Lily, Rose by John Singer Sargent.
Image from Tate Gallery, London/Art Resource, NY

WHAT IS A FRIEND?

La Rue Sanders

What is a friend? A friend is a bit of heaven lent to us to make earth a better place in which to live. He is a mirror which reflects a true picture of ourselves, unclouded and untouched. He is a window through which we see the world as it is, both the good and bad of it. A friend has all the beauty of the most beautiful rose, yet when left uncared for and neglected, slowly fades and dies. He has the strength one finds in a towering tree, but he, too, has to have regular nourishment for normal growth. Always in motion, he is much like the ocean, both feeding many smaller rivers and receiving the water which pours forth from them.

A friend is a forgotten path in the woods, stumbled upon quite by accident, but when followed, leads to the most attractive and restful place in the world. He has the wisdom of Solomon, the patience of Job, the courage of David, and the leadership of Moses. Yet he is just as human and just as sensitive as we are. He is expected to hear our troubles, solve our problems, understand and supply our needs, realize our faults but forgive and overlook them, accept our rebuffs, and then love us in spite of it all.

He is abused, misused, ignored, forgotten, and even cursed at times. But when the truth is revealed, he is the most needed, most sought after, and most loved of all God's creations . . . his beauty is as lasting as eternity, his smile sheds more light and warmth than does the sun, and his unspoken manner says, "I love you" much like the quiet benediction of a prayer.

The Bluebell Glade by Ernest Walbourn. Image from Fine Art Photographic Library Ltd./Courtesy of Beaton Brown Fine Paintings

*There is in friendship something of all relations,
and something above them all. It is the golden thread
that ties the heart of all the world.*

—John Evelyn

RARE FRIENDSHIP

George Matthew Adams

The older one grows, the more precious do one's friends become. In them, somehow, is centered so much of the lasting substance of all that makes life worthwhile.

I was reading from one of my favorite little books in which the author stated that a rare friendship was much more to be prized than rare love. He stated that it was found less often. I believe he is right.

Rare friendship has such reaching fingers. It doesn't demand; it keeps giving.

To own a friend is more than to own a castle or a great landed estate. And I believe there is a fine sense of ownership in friendships. Ownership without any demands or specified restrictions! It is founded first upon respect and understanding. And, as it ages, it grows more mellow and comforting.

Especially fine and inspiring is the friendship of one man toward another. It is possible to be so devoid of selfishness, whereas the friendship of a man for a woman is quite often tinged with this ele-

ment, though when it is not, it too enters into a rare state of beauty.

In a world where so many are ever seeking for place and wealth, to have and to hold a friend is to truly live.

Even in marriage this element must enter, else there is little happiness. Companionship and a true perspective of life's purposes are what hide behind this rare friendship of which I speak.

Open frankness, an ability to overlook and to appreciate, a desire to help and to live are what draw us near to the one we love in friendship.

The little candle that throws its beams in a dark room, flickering its light to those who need guidance, is no more remarkable than the little candles in the hearts of those who have lighted themselves, that their friends may more easily know just how to move in a very darkened world.

I can think of nothing finer than to be this sort of rare friend.

LETTER TO A FRIEND

Fra Giovanni

I salute you.

I am your friend, and my love for you goes deep. There is nothing I can give you which you have not got; but there is much, very much, that, while I cannot give it, you can take.

No heaven can come to us unless our hearts find rest in today. Take heaven! No peace lies in the future which is not hidden in this present little instance. Take peace! The gloom of the world is but a shadow. Behind it, yet within our reach, is joy! There is radiance and glory in the darkness, could we but see—and to see we only have to look . . . I beseech you to look.

Life is so full of meaning and purpose, so full of beauty—beneath its covering—that you will find earth but cloaks your heaven. Courage then to claim it, that is all! But courage you have, and the knowledge that we are pilgrims together, wending home through unknown country.

And so, I greet you with profound esteem and with the prayer that for you, now and forever, the day breaks, and the shadows flee away.

Les Fleurs du Printemps by Arthur Hacker. Image from
Fine Art Photographic Library Ltd./Waterhouse & Dodd

A CELEBRATION OF FRIENDSHIP

Insomuch as anyone pushes you nearer to God,
he or she is your friend.
—AUTHOR UNKNOWN

THE HIGHEST PLANE

William DeWitt Hyde

The highest plane, the best friends, are those with whom we consciously share the spiritual purpose of our lives. This highest friendship is as precious as it is rare. With such friends, we drop at once into a matter-of-course intimacy and communion. Nothing is held back; nothing is concealed; our aims are expressed with the assurance of sympathy; even our shortcomings are confessed with the certainty that they will be forgiven. Such friendship lasts as long as the virtue which is its common bond. Jealousy cannot come in to break it up. Absolute sincerity, absolute loyalty—these are the high terms on which such friendship must be held. A person may have many such friends on one condition: that he shall not talk to any one friend about what his friendship permits him to know of another friend. Each such relation must be complete within itself and hermetically sealed, so far as permitting anyone else to come inside the sacred circle of its mutual confidence. In such friendship, differences—as of age, sex, station in life—divide not, but rather enhance the sweetness and tenderness of the relationship. In Aristotle's words: "The friendship of the good, and of those who have the same virtues, is perfect friendship. Such friendship, therefore, endures so long as each retains his character, and virtue is a lasting thing."

For twenty-five years we have polished each other
like silver, with soft cloths, with loving attention.

THE TABLE AS ICON

Luci Shaw

How often Madeleine and I have sat at table together. The dining room table—where I used to live in West Chicago, or at my little house in Bellingham, or Madeleine's apartment in New York, or at Crosswicks Cottage—has been the setting for so many meals by candlelight, with linen and silver and flowers. As we sat there—either the two of us alone, or with other friends of the heart—always we were glad for such occasions of joy and celebration.

Perhaps the table which is, for me, the truest icon of our friendship is Madeleine's dining room table in New York City, worn to a mellow beauty that borrows not only from the candle flames and flowers but from the faces of all the friends who have gathered to partake of every meal there, served with grace and generosity (Madeleine is a superb cook), eaten with gratitude and gusto.

That table has also had another function. Often, during a day of editorial or proofreading work together, it has served as our editorial desk, piled with books and papers, decorated with rubber bands and paper clips. Even the cats are part of the creative clutter. Their favorite resting places are invariably the manuscripts we are working on *right now*. And if they're not napping on our brilliant ideas, they're rolling pen-cils along the surface, tapping them with delicately curled paws. Tatiana, the all-white princess, reclines at one end in regal splendor. Kelly and Terrible, the black-and-white duo, are more aggressive, arching their backs under our chins and curling their tails seductively around our necks, distracting us until we pick them up bodily from the table and lower them to the floor, firmly informing them that *that* is their place. Then, before dinner, we tidy up, set the table, and light the candles. We hold hands, singing the blessing before we begin to eat.

We both remember the first time we met for a meal, at my house near Wheaton, shortly after we met at Wheaton College. The occasion was a Language and Literature conference, and we were both participants. The conversation we began there has lasted a quarter of a century, and we both hope we have a similar span of time ahead of us. Our contact was never superficial; it started out, as it has continued, with God talk and book talk, the elements of the kind of friendship we both find the most satisfying. I gave Madeleine a copy of *Listen to the Green*, my first book of poems. She responded with *A Circle of Quiet*, and as I read it later I remember thinking, *How much we have in common! We both love to play Bach, we both need the tranquility of green space in woods, by streams; we both burn the peas when our minds are on loftier matters.*

In correspondence I learned that Madeleine's book of poetry *Lines Scribbled on an Envelope* had just gone out of print, and, publisher that I was, I asked her if she'd like us to reprint it, along with some of her more recent poems. When she responded with enthusiasm, our author/editor relationship had begun! Since then we have worked together on eight more of her books, starting with *Walking on Water*, her reflections on faith and art, which has continued to be a bestseller in the world that we both inhabit, where faith and art are both vital. The universe is itself a work of art, with God as the first Artist, the first Poet, and we both acknowledge our calling by this Maker to be co-creators, with God, with each other.

But the relationship soon transcended the professional. I had a classically Evangelical upbringing; Madeleine comes from an equally classical Episcopalian background. Our instruction and training in the Christian faith have been dramatically different. As we have both questioned, even doubted, and disagreed—without acrimony, though often with vigor—and reached together for deeper and truer understandings of God's ways with us, we have met in the middle, and nudged each other to continue to grow.

When my innate sacramentalism moved me, with my husband Harold, to enter the Episcopal church, and Madeleine and I began to share the holy food and drink at the Lord's table, we found that kneeling together at the altar was a profound and marvelous way of affirming love and friendship with each other and with our God.

Together we have shared the stresses and recompenses of parenthood; the drawn-out deaths by cancer of both our husbands, Harold and Hugh, in the same year; the rocky path of bereavement and grief which raised in both of us existential questions about the

Coffee Cups and Lilac by Piotr Stolerenko. Image from Fine Art Photographic Library Ltd./ Bourne Gallery, Reigate/Art Gallery Gerard, Wassenaar, Holland

meaning of life itself, and of our lives. These uncertainties have always led us to prayer, and prayer together, touching God, is, as Ecclesiastes tells us, a three-fold cord which is not quickly broken, a cord which thickens and strengthens with the years.

As we have passed together through both tragedy and triumph, through weakness and failure, we affirm that our friendship has not only been significant but that it has, on occasion, quite literally saved us in times of desperate need. This has required a degree of honesty with each other, which is the basis of true intimacy in a world where intimacy is often traded for superficiality. Last year I wrote in my journal:

> On the eve of departure from New York I just had time for my now customary polishing of Madeleine's candlesticks. Suddenly I realize I'm dealing with more than "just" candlesticks; I'm coming to think of it as "polishing Madeleine." Then I notice something I've missed before, her name (misspelled "Madeline") inscribed, faint but dark, on the base of two of the four silver candle-holders, and the idea of the polishing of a friend, and a friendship, turns even truer. It's a variation on the theme of the biblical proverb: "As iron sharpens iron, so the heart of friend with friend."
>
> Though we may need a kind of corrective sharpening from each other from time to time, polishing is a gentler art. As writers, critics, editors, wordsmiths, we polish each other's phrases and ideas. Yesterday I read Madeleine my new poem "Eucalyptus." After I'd fallen silent at the end of the poem, she said, without preamble, "Take off the last three lines." And she was absolutely right. Those lines were redundant, part of the scaffolding of the poem which needed to be peeled away to reveal the poem's central structure and integrity. So our roles of writer and editor reverse—often, easily, effortlessly. And we continue to luster each other to a shine in the joy of a friendship blessed by God.
>
> Beyond that, beyond the written or spoken work we produce are our very selves, our souls, the women we are in God. For twenty-five years we have polished each other like silver, with soft cloths, with loving attention. Birthday gifts fly between us in November and December. We celebrate on the 29th of those two months, ten years apart in chronology as we are. Daily phone calls punctuate times of stress or crisis, or to reassure and comfort. Letters, photographs, poems, flow through the mail. . . .

Vacations together open up new horizons for both of us. We've driven the Canadian Rockies and, together with our close friend Barbara, been pilgrims to Ireland and Iona and Lindisfarne. We've shopped Fortnum and Mason's in London, and boated across silver Lake Windermere between the green velvet hills of England's Lake District. These tales of travel all end up somewhere in a journal or a book or a poem, or serve as grist for reminiscence together.

And so the conversation continues—at the dining room table, the editorial desk, the Table of Communion, and, when we're in the mood for play, even the Ping-Pong table!

Spiced Creek by Natalie Levine. Image from Spiral Licensing

Dinner with Friends

Garlic Bread

2 garlic cloves

¼ teaspoon salt, or to taste

2 tablespoons unsalted butter, softened slightly

¼ cup olive oil

1 tablespoon minced fresh parsley leaves

1 12-inch whole-wheat baguette

1 12-inch white baguette

PREHEAT OVEN TO 375°F. In a small food processor or a blender, puree garlic with salt, butter, and oil until mixture is smooth. Transfer the mixture to a small bowl, and stir in parsley. Cut each baguette into 1-inch sections without cutting all the way through to the bottom. Spread some of the garlic mixture in each cut, and spread the remaining mixture on the tops of the baguettes. Wrap each baguette loosely in foil and bake 10 minutes. Open foil to expose the tops of the baguettes and bake 5 minutes more, or until hot and crusty. Makes 2 loaves.

Caesar Salad

2 flat anchovy fillets, or to taste, rinsed and drained

4 garlic cloves

2 teaspoons sherry vinegar

2 teaspoons fresh lemon juice

1 teaspoon Worcestershire sauce

½ teaspoon dry mustard

½ cup olive oil

4 heads of romaine, washed, spun dry, and torn into bite-size pieces (about 12 cups)

Croutons

Parmesan curls formed with a vegetable peeler

MINCE AND MASH THE ANCHOVIES with the garlic to form a paste. In a medium bowl, whisk together anchovy paste, vinegar, lemon juice, Worcestershire sauce, and mustard. Add oil in a stream, while whisking, and whisk the dressing until emulsified. In a large bowl, toss romaine with croutons and dressing; sprinkle Parmesan curls over salad. Makes 4 to 6 servings.

Enjoy a delicious meal with your close friends, sharing stories as you share food. Breaking bread together is one of the joys of deep friendship.

Swordfish with Angel Hair Pasta

1	pound angel hair pasta	2	large leeks, cut into rounds and separated
1½	pounds swordfish, cut into strips	3	tomatoes, peeled and chopped
¾	pound bay scallops	½	teaspoon thyme
3	tablespoons butter		Salt and black pepper to taste

COOK PASTA according to package directions; drain and set aside. Steam swordfish and scallops until fish flakes easily when tested, about 5 minutes. While fish steams, melt butter in a skillet over medium heat; add leeks and sauté until tender. Add tomatoes and cooked pasta; toss to mix. Season with thyme, salt, and pepper. Serve steamed fish and scallops over pasta. Makes 6 servings.

Caramel Flan

¾	cup granulated sugar	1	14-ounce can sweetened condensed milk
1	8-ounce package cream cheese, softened	1	12-ounce can evaporated milk
5	eggs	1	teaspoon vanilla extract

PREHEAT OVEN TO 350°F. In a small, heavy saucepan over medium-low heat, cook sugar, stirring, until golden. Pour into a 10-inch round baking dish, tilting to coat bottom and sides. Set aside. In a large bowl, beat cream cheese until smooth. Beat in eggs, one at a time, until well blended. Beat in condensed and evaporated milk and vanilla until smooth. Pour into caramel coated pan. Line a roasting pan with a kitchen towel. Place baking dish on towel, inside roasting pan, and place roasting pan on oven rack. Fill roasting pan with boiling water to reach halfway up the sides of the baking dish. Bake 50 to 60 minutes, until center is just set. Cool 1 hour on wire rack, then chill in refrigerator 8 hours or overnight. To unmold, run a knife around edges of pan and invert on a rimmed serving platter. Makes 10 servings.

Your Lamp of Friendship

FLORA C. ROSENBERG

Hold high your lamp of friendship
As you travel the rugged road;
Let it shine along the path
As I bear with grace my load.
Then strength will be given me
To endure with a cheery smile,
For your lamp will guide my feet
Along many a weary mile.

A FRIEND

Sandy Cayman

A friend is an inspiration, a guiding light, a helping hand. A friend is a companion and sympathizer, a supporter and well-wisher. A friend laughs with you, cries with you, and cares when sometimes you don't. He's a buddy and pal, the someone who often overlooks your faults and takes the blame himself. A friend cares for you and your well-being. He applauds your successes and helps pull you up by the bootstraps from life's failures. A friend has no knowledge of the word *obligation*, but, rather, complete understanding of generosity. A friend has a forgiving mind and a trusting, affectionate heart. A friend is a treasure of life.

A Helping Hand by Adrien Moreau.
Image from Fine Art Photographic
Library Ltd./Haynes Fine Art

INSPIRING EACH OTHER

Your Smile

LAURA L. ATKINS

There's a song in my heart, my friend,
There's a song in my heart today;
And it sings, and it sings,
And the glad music rings
All through the live-long day.
And the song that sings in my heart
Has a joyous and sweet melody;
'Tis because your smile
    makes the day worthwhile.
And so I am giving to others a smile,
Because you gave one to me.

Sunshine

A. C. SWINBURNE

My friend peers in on me with merry
Wise face; and, though the sky stay dim,
The very light of day—the very
Sun's self—comes in with him.

*A friend will strengthen you
with her prayers, bless you
with her love, and encourage
you with her heart.*
—AUTHOR UNKNOWN

Lilac Blossom by Viktor Yefimenko.
Image from Fine Art Photographic Library Ltd./ Bourne Gallery,
Reigate/Art Gallery Gerard, Wassenaar, Holland

THROUGH THICK AND THIN

Rejoice with those who rejoice;
mourn with those who mourn.
Live in harmony with one another.
—ROMANS 12:15–16 (NIV)

Rich or poor, young or old, we all need the
helping hands of friends from time to time.

WE ALL FALL DOWN

Pamela Kennedy

I have a playground duty for lunch recess. Sitting on a wooden bench, I watch as the elementary school girls jump rope, play tetherball, and spin Hula-Hoops around their waists. A few of them sit in a spot of shade, petting the big black cat that has lived at the school since anyone can remember. She laps up their attention like warm cream and rubs her whiskered chin against their knobby knees, begging for more. In the far corner of the playground, a group of four kindergartners clasp hands and dance in a jerky circle singing, "Ring around the rosies, pocket full of posies, ashes, ashes, we all fall down!" Then they collapse, laughing, on the grass.

I smile remembering when I was only five and I sang the same song, dancing in a circle with my friends. It was funny to fall down when we were little. We got up so quickly then. But my thoughts skip along the years, remembering other times of falling, times when getting up was difficult or even seemed impossible, times when I needed the hands of friends to reach out in love and help me to my feet again.

As a young mother, I felt unqualified and inept on so many days. Once, my preschooler ate a handful of toadstools from a neighbor's front yard, and I had to rush him to the hospital emergency room. As I sat there, afraid, feeling like a bad mother, waiting for the ipecac to work, a friend showed up. She didn't say much, but she sat beside me and held my hand until my little boy was better. I remember other times when, exhausted from lack of sleep or frustrated by a cranky child, I lost my perspective on parenting in general and fell into despair. Then good friends offered encouragement, support, words of wisdom, or just a listening ear and lifted me back up.

Sometimes at work, when deadlines loomed, when days passed and things piled up, I felt almost as though I were slowly sinking in a pit. I feared I'd fail, that I'd disappoint my boss. Then good friends reached out, lifting burdens, finding solutions, and helping me back onto the solid ground of accomplishment.

Sometimes the deep places I landed in were of my own making, but friends don't condemn and judge, they just offer their helping hands. Other times the circumstances of life, illness, and loneliness dragged me to my knees and there I'd sit until some kind friend came beside me, offered her hand, and helped me to my feet again.

A CELEBRATION OF FRIENDSHIP

Rich or poor, young or old, we all need the helping hands of friends from time to time. Solomon, the richest king who ever lived, must have understood this when he wrote the famous lines in Ecclesiastes. He must have realized that wealth and fame are cold company when one lies in the dust of despair.

But I wonder if Solomon recognized the other side of his words of wisdom. As wonderful as it is to receive a helping hand, it is equally rewarding to offer one. Each day brings so many opportunities to be a person of encouragement. In any single day, there are people we encounter who have fallen down. There's the single mother who needs a hand watching her children so she can run an errand or have a quiet moment to herself. When someone is ill or grieving, a warm meal or a short visit can lift the spirits and help ease the pain. There are little children who would love to hear a story read, older neighbors who'd love to tell one, people who have broken things in need of mending, and those who desperately long for simple conversation. Life is filled with hands and hearts reaching out for ours.

The recess bell rings and the children put away their jumping ropes. The tetherball swings around the pole listlessly; the black cat stretches and then wanders toward a puddle of sunshine for a nap. The kindergartners line up and march behind their teachers to their classrooms, but I still sit on the green wooden bench and hear

their song. Will they remember, I wonder, to hold tightly to one another's hands? For as we dance through the circles of our lives, there are so many times when we all fall down.

The Daisy Chain by Florence Fitzgerald. Image from Fine Art Photographic Library Ltd./Courtesy of Christopher Cole Paintings, Beaconsfield

THROUGH THICK AND THIN

You Call Me Friend

HILDA BUTLER FARR

You call me friend,
But do you realize
How much the name implies?
It means that down the years,
Through sunshine and through tears,
There's always someone standing by your heart.
You call me friend,
And thus your life and mine
Grow richer in design.
And I would have you know,
Wherever you may go,
There's always someone standing by your heart.

TWO ARE BETTER

Ecclesiastes 4:9–12

Two are better than one; because they have a good reward for their labour. For if they fall, the one will lift up his fellow: but woe to him that is alone when he falleth; for he hath not another to help him up. Again, if two lie together, then they have heat: but how can one be warm alone? And if one prevail against him, two shall withstand him; and a threefold cord is not quickly broken.

Friendship improves happiness, and abates misery, by doubling our joy, and dividing our grief.

—JOSEPH ADDISON

Summer Playmates by Alexander Tioutrine. Image from Fine Art Photographic Library Ltd./ Bourne Gallery, Reigate/Art Gallery Gerard, Wassenaar, Holland

That's What Friends Are For

Carole Bayer Sager

Burt F. Bacharach

And I nev-er thought I'd feel this way; and, as

far as I'm concerned, I'm glad I got the chance to say that I

do be-lieve I love you. And if I should ev-er go a-way, well, then

close your eyes and try to feel the way we do to-day. And then

if you can re- mem-ber: Keep smil - ing, keep shin - ing,

know-ing you can al-ways count on me for sure;

that's what friends are for. For good times and bad times, I'll be on your

side for - ev - er more. That's what friends are for.

Constant use had not worn ragged
the fabric of their friendship.
—DOROTHY PARKER

THE TRUE FRIEND

Harry Halsey Starrett

The true friend stands ever ready to heed every call for help, but never intrudes; and when his mission has been fulfilled, he silently withdraws, always mindful and respectful of the sanctity of the divine heritage of freedom of those whom he befriends.

The true friend helps without any thought of personal praise or profit, not that he many aggrandize and immortalize himself in the hearts of the people, but that he may fulfill the law of righteousness.

To the true friend, it matters not whether those he serves are grateful or ungrateful—he just moves about, doing good for good's sake only. Faithfulness is the guiding principle of the true friend.

I do not wish to treat friendships
daintily, but with roughest courage.
When they are real, they are not
glass threads or frost-work,
but the solidest thing we know.
—RALPH WALDO EMERSON

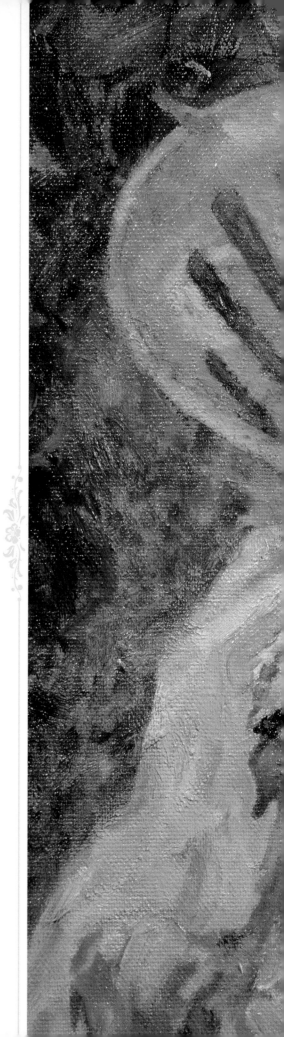

The Chocolate Biscuit by Guerennadi Bernadsky.
Image from Fine Art Photographic Library Ltd./Bourne Gallery,
Reigate/Art Gallery Gerard, Wassenaar, Holland

*It is not that a man has occasion often to fall back
upon the kindness of his friends; perhaps he may never
experience the necessity of doing so; but we are governed
by our imaginations, and they stand there as a solid and
impregnable bulwark against all the evils of life.*
—SYDNEY SMITH

ON FRIENDSHIP AND MATERIAL ADVANTAGE

Marcus Tullius Cicero

It has very often occurred to me when thinking about friendship that the chief point to be considered was this: is it weakness and want of means that make friendship desired? I mean, is its object an interchange of good offices, so that each may give that in which he is strong and receive that in which he is weak? Or is it not rather true that, although this is an advantage naturally belonging to friendship, yet its original cause is quite other, prior in time, more noble in character, and springing more directly from our nature itself? The Latin word for friendship—*amicitia*—is derived from that for love—*amor*; and love is certainly the prime mover in contracting mutual affection. . . .

For as we are not beneficent and liberal with any view of extorting gratitude and do not regard an act of kindness as an investment, but follow a natural inclination to liberality; so we look on friendship as worth trying for, not because we are attracted to it by the expectation of ulterior gain, but in the conviction that what it has to give us is from first to last included in the feeling itself. . . .

Indeed I am inclined to think that friends ought at times to be in want of something. For instance, what scope would my affections have had if Scipio had never wanted my advice or cooperation at home or abroad? It is not friendship, then, that follows material advantage, but material advantage, friendship.

Elegant Women on a Beach by Isidore Verheyden.
Image from Christie's Images Ltd.

✦ III ✦
THROUGH THICK AND THIN

Kindred Hearts

FELICIA HEMANS

O ask not, hope thou not, too much
Of sympathy below;
Few are the hearts whence one same touch
Bids the sweet fountains flow:
Few—and by still conflicting powers
Forbidden here to meet—
Such ties would make this life of ours
Too fair for aught so fleet.

It may be that thy brother's eye
Sees not as thine, which turns
In such deep reverence to the sky,
Where the rich sunset burns;
It may be that the breath of spring,
Born amidst violets lone,
A rapture o'er thy soul can bring—
A dream, to his unknown.

The tune that speaks of other times—
A sorrowful delight!
The melody of distant chimes,
The sound of waves by night;

The wind that, with so many a tone,
Some chord within can thrill—
These may have language all thine own,
To him a mystery still.

Yet scorn thou not, for this, the true
And steadfast love of years;
The kindly, that from childhood grew,
The faithful to thy tears!
If there be one that o'er the dead
Hath in thy grief borne part,
And watch'd through sickness by thy bed—
Call his a kindred heart!

But for those bonds all perfect made,
Wherein bright spirits blend,
Like sister flowers of one sweet shade
With the same breeze that bend;
For that full bliss of thought allied,
Never to mortals given—
O lay thy lovely dreams aside,
Or lift them unto heaven!

*Friendship that flows from the heart cannot be frozen by adversity,
as the water that flows from the spring cannot congeal in winter.*

—JAMES FENIMORE COOPER

Through Thick and Thin

GRIEF LIKE A SHAWL

Karla Dornacher

I have a friend who endured a terrible loss. Her grief clung to her like a heavy shawl around her shoulders. I could not take the shawl from her, but I could come alongside her and lift a corner of that shawl upon myself to help her bear its weight. More than once she apologized for being a burden, but I assured her— that's what friends are for.

It's not always easy, at least for me, to develop the ability to listen and embrace without offering advice or correction and without sharing my own equally traumatic experiences. And I must confess that there were moments that I wanted her to put it behind her. I yearned for days to come when we would share more joy than sorrow. But grief must be walked out, step by tearful step.

The Bible tells us that we are not to grow weary in doing good because joy returns to those who wait patiently on the Lord! Never quit praying and never give up . . . on your friend or your God!

There is a time to speak, to embrace, and to encourage. And there is a time to quietly come alongside, lift the shawl, and be a friend.

As a relationship matures, you start to see that just being there for each other is the most important thing you can do: just being there to listen and be sorry with them, to be happy with them, to share all that there is to share.

—FRED ROGERS

God . . . laid a mantle of order, beauty, and loving care into our home through these four "angels."

THE LOVE SQUAD

Virelle Kidder

"Oh, no! Not company!" I groaned the moment that my car rounded the corner and our house came into full view. Usually I'd be thrilled to see four cars lined up in our driveway, but after I spent a week-long vigil at the hospital with an ill child, my house was a colossal mess. Turning off the car engine, I dragged myself to the door.

"What are you doing home so soon?" my friend Judie called from the kitchen. "We weren't expecting you for another hour! We thought we'd be long gone before you got home." She walked toward me and gave me a hug, then asked softly, "How are you doing?"

Was this my house? Was I dreaming? Everything looked so clean. Where did these flowers come from?

Suddenly more voices, more hugs. Lorraine, smiling and wiping beads of perspiration from her forehead, came up from the family room where she had just finished ironing a mountain of clean clothes. Regina peeked into the kitchen, having finished vacuuming rugs and polishing and dusting furniture in every room in the house. Joan, still upstairs wrestling with the boys' bunk-bed sheets, called down her hello, having already brought order out of chaos in all four bedrooms.

"When did you guys get here?" was my last coherent sentence. My tears came in great heaving waves. "How come . . . how come . . . you did all this?" I cried unashamedly, every ounce of resistance gone.

I had spent the week praying through a health crisis, begging God for a sense of his presence at the hospital. Instead, he laid a mantle of order, beauty, and loving care into our home through these four "angels."

"You rest a while, Virelle," Lorraine said firmly. "Here's your dinner for tonight—there are more meals in the freezer." The table was set with flowers and fancy napkins, and a little gift was at my place. A small banquet was arranged, complete with salad and dessert.

"Don't you worry. We're all praying," my friends said. "God has everything under control."

After my friends left, I wandered from room to room, still sobbing from the enormity of their gift of time and work. I found beautiful floral arrangements in every room . . . and little wrapped gifts on each bed. More tears.

In the living room I found a note under a vase filled with peonies. I was to have come home and found it as their only identity: "The Love Squad was here."

And I *knew* that God had everything under control.

Coffee on the Terrace by Piotr Stolerenko. Image from Fine Art Photographic Library Ltd./ Bourne Gallery, Reigate/Art Gallery Gerard, Wassenaar, Holland

SOUPS TO SHARE

Garden Chili

2 tablespoons olive oil
1 zucchini, sliced
1 yellow squash, sliced
1 red bell pepper, diced
1 green bell pepper, diced
1 fresh jalapeno pepper, diced
4 cloves garlic, minced
1 onion, chopped
1 28-ounce can crushed
   tomatoes, with liquid

1 6-ounce can tomato paste
1 15-ounce can black beans, drained
   and rinsed
1 15.25-ounce can whole kernel corn, drained
1 15-ounce can chili beans in
   spicy sauce, undrained
1 tablespoon chili powder
½ teaspoon dried oregano
½ teaspoon black pepper
¼ teaspoon cayenne pepper, or to taste

IN A LARGE POT over medium-high heat, heat oil. Stir in zucchini, yellow squash, red bell pepper, green bell pepper, jalapeno, garlic, and onion. Cook 5 minutes, just until tender. Add tomatoes, tomato paste, black beans, corn, and chili beans. Season with chili powder, oregano, black pepper, and cayenne pepper. Bring to a boil. Reduce heat to low and simmer 1 hour, stirring occasionally.

Campfire Stew

¾ cup butter or margarine
1½ pounds onions, sliced
1 teaspoon caraway seed
1 small clove garlic, crushed
1 tablespoon paprika

3 pounds beef chuck or rump, cubed
1½ cups water
   Salt to taste
3 green peppers, seeded and
   cut in chunks

IN A DUTCH OVEN over medium heat, melt butter and sauté onions until tender and golden brown in color. Add seasonings. Add beef cubes and enough water to cover. Salt to taste. Cover and simmer gently until meat is tender. Add more watter if necessary. Stir in green peppers during last half hour. Makes 6 to 8 servings.

Perfect for serving to friends in somber or joyous circumstances, these comforting, relaxed soups are sure to warm the hearts of those you hold dear.

Tuscan Vegetable Soup

1 tablespoon olive oil	2 cups diced carrots
1½ cups finely chopped onion	8 cups low-sodium chicken broth
1½ teaspoons dried or 2 tablespoons chopped fresh thyme	3 cups diced potato
3 teaspoons minced garlic	½ cup chopped fresh basil
4 cups coarsely chopped green cabbage	3 cups half-slices of zucchini (cut zucchini in half lengthwise, then cut into slices)
1 14.5-ounce can Italian-style stewed tomatoes, with liquid	1 15-ounce can red kidney beans, rinsed and drained
2 cups sliced celery	6 tablespoons shredded Parmesan cheese

IN A LARGE, NONSTICK SAUCEPAN over medium heat, heat olive oil . Add onion, thyme, and garlic; sauté 3 to 5 minutes. Stir in cabbage, tomatoes, celery, and carrots; sauté 8 to 10 minutes. Stir in the chicken broth, potatoes, basil, zucchini, and kidney beans; bring to a boil. Reduce heat to simmer; cover saucepan and simmer about 1 hour. Serve hot. Top each serving with a tablespoon of Parmesan cheese. Makes 6 large servings.

Summer Squash Soup

3 cups chopped uncooked yellow summer squash	1 tablespoon flour
3 cups milk	1 tablespoon vegetable oil
½ cup dry skim milk powder	2 tablespoons brown sugar
1 tablespoon minced parsley	1 teaspoon salt
2 cups water	Chopped parsley

COOK SQUASH in salted water until soft. Cool slightly. Drain. Rub through sieve or mash. In a large pot, combine with other ingredients. Bring to a boil over medium heat. Simmer 10 minutes. Serve hot. Garnish with chopped parsley. Makes 4 servings.

Friends in Need

ESTELLE TAYLOR

I came to you with troubled heart;
    I knew not what—
Evil, fear, imagination—had played their part.
Your tender care—your quiet thought—
    renewed the strength,
Courage, hope, and faith I sought.

But when you bared your heart to me,
    mountains of love
Arose to help you crown a victory.
'Twas then my troubles melted as the
    brightening sun
Swallows the darkness;
With unfaltering step, renewed life was begun.
And now I know it was to be;
Time tempers all:
I needed you—you needed me.

*[Friendship] is for aid and
comfort through all the relations
and passages of life and death.
It is fit for serene days and
graceful gifts and country
rambles, but also for rough
roads and hard fare, shipwreck,
poverty, and persecution.*
—RALPH WALDO EMERSON

In the Meadow by William Affleck. Image from
Fine Art Photographic Library Ltd./Waterhouse & Dodd

Friendship

AUTHOR UNKNOWN

Friendship needs no studied phrases,
Polished face, or winning wiles;
Friendship deals no lavish praises;
Friendship dons no surface smiles.

Friendship follows nature's diction,
Shuns the blandishments of art,
Boldly severs truth from fiction,
Speaks the language of the heart.

Friendship favors no condition,
Scorns a narrow-minded creed,
Lovingly fulfills its mission,
Be it word or be it deed.

Friendship cheers the faint and weary,
Makes the timid spirit brave,
Warns the erring, lights the dreary,
Smoothes the passage to the grave.

Friendship—pure, unselfish friendship—
All through life's allotted span,
Nurtures, strengthens, widens lengthens,
Man's relationship with man.

The tide of friendship does not rise high on the
banks of perfection. Amiable weaknesses and shortcomings
are the food of love. . . . My friends are not perfect,
no more than I, and so we suit each other admirably.
It is one of the charitable dispensations of
Providence that perfection is not essential to friendship.

—ALEXANDER SMITH

The Arrow
and the Song

HENRY WADSWORTH LONGFELLOW

I shot an arrow into the air;
It fell to earth, I know not where;
For, so swiftly it flew, the sight
Could not follow it in its flight.

I breathed a song into the air;
It fell to earth, I knew not where;
For who has sight so keen and strong,
That it can follow the flight of song?

Long, long afterward, in an oak
I found the arrow, still unbroke;
And the song, from beginning to end,
I found again in the heart of a friend.

THE TRUE ATMOSPHERE
OF FRIENDSHIP

Randolph Bourne

The true atmosphere of friendship is a sunny one. Griefs and disappointments do not thrive in its clear, healthy light. When they do appear, they take on a new color. The silver lining appears, and we see even our own personal mistakes and chagrins as whimsical adventures. It is almost impossible seriously to believe in one's bad luck or failures or incapacity while one is talking with a friend. One achieves a sort of transfiguration of personality in those moments.

Playing with a Hoop by Victor Gabriel Gilbert.
Image from Fine Art Photographic Library Ltd./
Courtesy of Mensing Gallery, Hamm-Rhynern, Germany

FOREVER FRIENDS

We have been friends together,
In sunshine and in shade,
Since first beneath the chestnut trees
In infancy we played.
—CAROLINE ELIZABETH SARAH NORTON

*I realized we had more to give to one
another than ever. More than ever, I appreciated
the friendship that had survived so many years.*

MORE THAN EVER

Harriet May Savitz

We had not seen each other for thirty years. Neither of us knew how that had happened. We had been dear friends when we were fourteen years old and through our teenage and young-married years. Somehow, life had tossed us about in different directions. But we never forgot one another.

Now we were getting together again. She was still married to the man she had fallen in love with, and I was now a widow. She came east to attend a wedding, and while she was here, we planned a visit. So many years had intervened. So much of life had already been lived. I wondered, *How could we catch up with all of it? Would there be enough time? Was the distance too long between the young girls who giggled all afternoon while listening to the phonograph, and the mothers and grandmothers we now were?*

Looking back, the problems we shared then, so urgent at the time, appeared less so now. Hours spent wondering if our bodies would ever change so that young men would be attracted to their curves. And when they did, other problems arrived. As we sat and painted fingernails together, daydreamed together, decided on the Saturday night date together, shopped for clothes together, we knew instinctively we could

deal with all the changes, the frustrations, and the uncertainties together. I traveled nearly an hour to spend Sunday mornings in her kitchen having breakfast with her parents. They never knew why we were laughing or what we talked about at the table. She came to the shore to be with me, to sit on the sand, baking for hours, but with the silent understanding we didn't dare go in the water and get wet. That would have been disastrous to the image we had spent hours creating. To the world, we were popular and fun. To each other, we were real. Vulnerable and unsure.

We had seen each other last in the midst of life, children about our knees, energy in our eyes. I was thinking just before she arrived, *Would she not recognize me now?* I glanced into the mirror and surveyed the white hair, the lined face. *Would she be doing the same?*

When she stepped from the car, we spent many long moments just looking at one another. I knew then that it didn't matter what we looked like. For neither of us would see it, anyway. "You look the same," I said, and I meant it. She said something similar to me. For in our laugh, our broad smiles, our loving eyes and warm hugs, nothing had changed.

Perhaps because love is ageless. And that's what had remained between us, the strong bond of friendship and the love that accompanied it. We both felt its power as we stood there, for those few moments in silence, just drinking in each other's presence.

She had kept our friendship alive through photographs, which she shared. One was of me in a bathing suit. On the back I had written that someday we would sit together, perhaps fifty years later, and my love for her would be the same. And it was over fifty years later that we were doing so. But my feelings were even deeper now. Sitting at my kitchen table—sharing tea and cake, talking about our children and grandchildren, our accomplishments in life—I realized we had more to give to one another than ever. More than ever, I appreciated the friendship that had survived so many years.

We laughed over the moment, on a street corner after we had attended our college night classes, when she told me that she and the wonderful young man she loved were going to get married. "Married?" I asked, shocked. "You don't want to get married. Not yet." She was about twenty. And so was I. We were going to college at night. We had dreams to chase, together. Now she would seek them with someone else, and leave me to chase them alone.

Fifty years later, as the back of the photograph predicted, we were sitting around a table. It also predicted we wouldn't look the same.

To each other, we did.

News from Abroad by Henry John Yeend King. Image from Fine Art Photographic Library Ltd./Courtesy of Haynes Fine Art, Broadway

One Sister Have I in Our House

EMILY DICKINSON

One sister have I in our house,
And one a hedge away;
There's only one recorded
But both belong to me.

One came the way that I came
And wore my past year's gown;
The other as a bird her nest,
Builded our hearts among.

She did not sing as we did;
It was a different tune,
Herself to her a music,
As bumblebee of June.

Today is far from childhood,
But up and down the hills
I held her hand the tighter,
Which shortened all the miles.

And still her hum the years among
Decieves the butterfly;
Still in her eyes the violets lie
Mouldered these many May.

I spilt the dew but took the morn;
I chose this single star
From out the wide night's numbers,
Sue—forevermore!

*We've been friends forever. I suppose that can't be true.
There must have been a time before we became friends,
but I can't remember it. You are in my first memory
and all my best memories ever since.*
—LINDA MACFARLANE

A Picnic Together

Chicken Salad Sandwiches

4 cups cubed cooked chicken
   (about 1¾ lb)

1 cup walnuts, toasted and chopped

1 celery rib, cut into ¼-inch-thick
   slices (1 cup)

2 tablespoons finely chopped shallot

2 cups halved seedless red grapes

¾ cup mayonnaise

3 tablespoons tarragon vinegar

2 tablespoons finely chopped
   fresh tarragon

½ teaspoon salt

½ teaspoon black pepper
   Slices of sandwich bread

IN A LARGE BOWL, toss together all ingredients but bread until well combined. Spread between slices of bread for sandwiches. Refrigerate if not serving immediately. Makes 4 to 6 servings.

Macaroni Fruit Salad with Orange Dressing

1 8-ounce package elbow macaroni

½ cup wheat germ, divided

1 15-ounce can pineapple tidbits

1 cup cantaloupe balls

1 4-ounce can mandarin orange
   segments, drained

1 cup seedless grape halves

1 cup mandarin orange
   flavored yogurt

2 tablespoons honey
   Salad greens, optional

COOK MACARONI according to package directions. Drain and transfer to a large bowl. Reserve 2 tablespoons wheat germ. Sprinkle remaining wheat germ over macaroni; blend well. Drain pineapple tidbits, reserving juice. Add pineapple, cantaloupe, oranges, and grapes to macaroni; toss lightly. In a small bowl, combine 2 tablespoons of the reserved pineapple juice, yogurt, and honey; blend well. Pour yogurt dressing over fruit and macaroni; toss until well coated. Sprinkle reserved wheat germ over top of salad. Chill about 2 hours. Serve on crisp salad greens, if desired.

Pack a picnic basket or just set a backyard table, and invite old friends for a relaxed meal in the great outdoors.

Deluxe Potato Salad

8 medium potatoes or 12 new potatoes	4 hard-boiled eggs, diced
1 10.5-ounce can chicken broth	Chopped parsley
1 large red onion, minced	Salt and pepper
12 cherry tomatoes	1 cup mayonnaise or
1 4-ounce can artichoke hearts, drained and sliced	salad dressing

IN A LARGE POT, boil potatoes in their skins until tender, about 25 minutes; drain and set aside until cool. Peel and slice potatoes; transfer to a large bowl. Pour chicken broth over potatoes; let stand for 1 hour. In a large serving bowl, combine onion, tomatoes, artichoke hearts, and eggs. Sprinkle on parsley, salt, and pepper to taste. Just before serving, drain potatoes and add to vegetables; toss lightly. Stir in mayonnaise. Refrigerate if not serving immediately. If transporting, keep potato salad well chilled. Makes 6 to 8 servings.

Rich Strawberry Ice Cream

6 egg yolks	1 tablespoon vanilla
2 cups granulated sugar, divided	3½ cups heavy cream
½ teaspoon salt	2 pints strawberries, hulled, washed,
3 cups milk, scalded	drained, and mashed

IN A MEDIUM BOWL, beat together egg yolks, 1 cup sugar, and salt. Slowly stir in scalded milk. Pour into medium saucepan and cook over medium heat until mixture coats a metal spoon. Remove from heat; add vanilla and cool. Stir in cream; cover and chill. Meanwhile, stir remaining sugar into mashed strawberries (if sugared frozen berries substituted, do not add sugar); let stand several hours. Combine strawberries and chilled custard. Pour into container of drum-type freezer and proceed according to manufacturer's instructions for freezing ice cream. Makes 4 quarts.

THE LONG CONVERSATION

Ellen Goodman and Patricia O'Brien

It amazes us now to look back and see what we've been building: the story of our friendship is the story of our divorces, our children, careers, loves, losses, remarriages, knee injuries, and even our differing opinions on such earth-shattering matters as pickles and olives. At a dozen times, we might have taken a different course without each other's advice—wrecked a love affair, accepted the wrong job, or made the wrong decision for a child.

We knew precisely how important this ongoing conversation, this running commentary, was to the person each of us had become. But it was a bit of a jolt to recognize that we had become the joint owners of a respectably long and grounded friendship. We had moved from youth through middle age with each other, becoming stronger than we would have been alone. We had talked and talked and talked, and finally talked our way through a quarter of a century—and in that time, we had become fluent in the language of female friendship.

Some people come into
our lives and quickly go.
Some people stay for a while and
leave their footprints on our hearts,
and we are never, ever the same.
—FLAVIA WEEDN

Sunlight and Shadow in the Garden by Piotr Stolerenko. Image from
Fine Art Photographic Library Ltd./Bourne Gallery, Reigate/
Art Gallery Gerard, Wassenaar, Holland

To Richard Watson Gilder

AUSTIN DOBSON

Old friends are best! And so to you
Again I send, in closer throng,
No unfamiliar shapes of song,
But those that once you liked and knew.
You surely will not do them wrong;
For are you not an old friend too?
Old friends are best.

Old books, old wine, old Nankin blue—
All things, in short, to which belong
The charm, the grace that time
     makes strong—
All these I prize, but (*entre nous*)
Old friends are best!

*Old friends are the real blessing of one's latter years.
Half a word conveys one's meaning. They have a memory
of the same events and have the same mode of thinking.
I have young relations that may grow upon me,
for my nature is affectionate, but can they grow old friends?*
—HORACE WALPOLE

Salt of the Earth

AUTHOR UNKNOWN

New friends I cherish and treasure their worth,
But old friends to me are the salt of the earth.
Friends are like garments that everyone wears—
New ones are needed for dress-up affairs;
But when we're at leisure, we're more apt to choose
The clothes that we purchased with last season's shoes.

Things we grow used to are things we love best—
The ones we are certain have weathered the test.
And isn't it true, since we're talking of friends,
That new ones bring pleasure when everything blends?
But when we want someone who thinks as we do,
And who fits, as I said, like last summer's shoe,
We turn to the friends who have stuck through the years,
Who echo our laughter and dry up our tears;
They know every weakness and fault we possess,
But somehow forget them in friendship's caress.

The story is old, yet fragrant and sweet;
I've said it before, but just let me repeat:
New friends I cherish and treasury their worth,
But old friends to me are the salt of the earth.

*Old friends are best. King James
used to call for his old shoes:
they were easiest for his feet.*

—JOHN SELDEN

These friendships, full of love and affirmation,
fortify my adult life, providing oxygen,
color, and texture.

PHOTOGRAPHS

Sharon J. Wohlmuth

In the room in one's brain where memories are stored, I find it difficult to retrieve images of myself as a young child playing with a best friend.

Nor can I search and retrieve from boxes of old childhood photographs many images of myself smiling into the camera with my arms wrapped around a best friend. In most of the photographs, I am with my relatives—cousins, aunts, and uncles at our Sunday family gatherings.

Yet there are dozens of pictures of my sister, Beth, and her best friend, Joanie, our neighbor—toothy three-year-olds embracing in Halloween costumes; and now, forty years later, still with their arms around each other at Beth's son's bar mitzvah. Their friendship over the years has become as well worn as the path that connected our backyards.

Why there are so few pictures of my own childhood friends doesn't really seem important to me now.

I realize as an adult that, unknowingly, my own journey to friendship began with a two-hundred-year-old oak tree that stood between my parents' and our neighbors' houses, dominating the landscape.

The oak provided the perfect "home" for the games of hide-and-seek that we used to play. I loved the texture of its worn bark. The massive trunk, too large for me to wrap my arms around, represented permanence and security.

My friends today remind me of that oak.

Now my arms reach all the way around, and my friends embrace me back. These friendships, full of love and affirmation, fortify my adult life, providing oxygen, color, and texture. I look at my friends countless times every day, for photographs of them spill across my refrigerator door.

FOREVER FRIENDS

A best friend is a safe harbor,
a guaranteed comfort zone.

BEST FRIENDS

Carol Saline

I know what it means to have best friends. My friendships—several of thirty and forty years' duration—are the food and water that nourish my life. Once someone joins my intimate circle, I'm positively tenacious about keeping them in my loving grip.

Oh yes, I know what it means to have best friends. Let me tell you about Roz and Elaine.

"Ra Rut," as I used to call her, came into my life when I was three years old and her family moved into the identical row house directly across the street. One day she pushed me off my tricycle. I immediately forgave her. We've been best friends ever since. As children, we talked about linking our houses with tin cans and string, but we never bothered because the only time we were apart was while we slept.

Our one and only major fight occurred when I lost the election for president of our high school sorority—and Roz won. I was utterly devastated that my best friend would oppose me. Friends aren't supposed to do that! But within a few days, something in my adolescent anguish realized that being friends with Roz mattered more to me than being angry with her. At some unspoken level, I think I recognized that if she wanted something as badly as I did, we both had the right to go for it. There had

always been a subtle competition between us. Wherever one of us set the bar, the other strove to match the standard. But rather than creating friction, our rivalry stimulated our personal growth.

We are a living history of each other's lives. Fortunately, our interests and lifestyles have developed along similar lines. One reason our friendship has remained vibrant for so long is that we never outgrew each other. We have grieved together for the loss of parents, and celebrated every joyous occasion from our own fourth birthdays to the fourth birthdays of our grandchildren. Roz is not my family—but she might as well be.

The last thirty-something years of our friendship have included Elaine, who slipped in with us when she and Roz became neighbors in 1962. We leaned on each other as we muddled through child rearing, adjusted to the demands of marriage, and tried to figure out what to do with our college-educated dreams. In the year we all turned fifty, Elaine was stricken with a brain tumor, which, thank God, turned out to be benign. Roz and I convinced the doctor to allow us into the recovery room when she came out of anesthesia. As we stood by her bed, placing ice chips in her mouth and mopping her brow with compresses, we recognized that we were as committed in our devotion to each other as any bride and groom reciting their marriage vows.

While we three don't have childhood memories in common, we weathered the critical years of adulthood in an inextricable intimacy. No one knows my secrets like they do, and no one's advice has been more caring or valuable.

Because of them, my wonderful sister Patsy, and a handful of others, I have come to learn that what matters in life is having best friends.

A best friend is a safe harbor, a guaranteed comfort zone. You never have to explain yourself to a best friend because they really, really know who you are. With a best friend, you can drop your guard and let down your hair. You can cry too hard or laugh too loud and never worry what they'll think of you. Because best friends are *nonjudgmental*. They will supply you with feedback or advice if you want it and a kick in the pants if you need it, but a best friend will not stand in judgment or make you ashamed of your behavior. A best friend gives you what you expect from a parent and don't always get: *unconditional love*.

Meadowsweet by Viktor Yefimenko. Image from Fine Art Photographic Library Ltd./ Bourne Gallery, Reigate/Art Gallery Gerard, Wassenaar, Holland

FOREVER FRIEND

Wilma Echols

My friend, many times have I spoken to you in this last year and, once again, I would speak to you of something my heart would have you know and remember for the rest of your life, in this world where men grow so tired and lonely. I would tell you that, in this world of ours, we meet many people whom we call our friends. We receive so much from these people with whom our pathways cross. We receive from them that which is good, and we give to them that which is good in us. But people, good and bad alike, come and go.

If we are lucky, as you and I have been upon our pathway of life, we happen to meet one who is destined to be a "forever friend." I have been so fortunate . . . I met you. You know me so well, even as I also know you. When my heart cries out for the "at-homeness" friend; the friend who feels my heartbeat; the friend who has seen me plod slowly; who has seen me riding high on the ferris wheel of life; who has laughed with me, cried with me; who loves me, even just as I am with all my shortcomings, my victories, and my defeats; who listens to me, hearing that which is good and casting away that which is bad; when my heart aches for the "old shoe" comfort, refreshing as the spring rain, then my heart aches for my "forever friend."

And though she be as near as my back door, or as far away as the four corners of the world, I know that she is only one heartbeat away. I would that she should know that, in my heart, she dwells in a spot set apart for her alone, as my "forever friend" . . . there now, always, and forevermore.

Poppy Fields by Henry John Yeend King.
Image from Fine Art Photographic Library Ltd./Walker Gallery

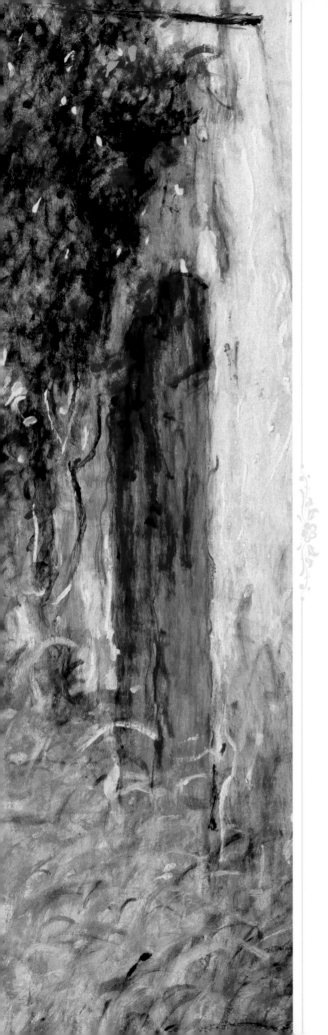

It Is a Sweet Thing

PERCY BYSSHE SHELLEY

It is a sweet thing, friendship: a dear balm;
A happy and auspicious bird of calm
Which rides o'er life's ever-tumultuous ocean;
A god that broods over chaos in commotion;
A flower which, fresh as Lapland roses are,
Lifts its bold head into the world's frore air
And blooms most radiantly when others die—
Health, hope, and youth, and brief prosperity—
And with the light and odor of its bloom,
Shining within the dungeon and the tomb,
Whose coming is as light and music are
Amid dissonance and loom; a star
Which moves not mid the moving heavens alone;
A smile amid dark frowns; a gentle tone
Among rude voices; a beloved light,
A solitude, a refuge, a delight.

My coat and I live comfortably together. It has assumed all my wrinkles, does not hurt me anywhere, has molded itself on my deformities, and is complacent to all my movements; and I only feel its presence because it keeps me warm. Old coats and old friends are the same thing.

—VICTOR HUGO

Conversation by Claude Fossoux. Image from Spiral Licensing

Seeing one another at our best and worst
has created an unconditional love and a bond
that's grown deeper as we've moved from
children to adults, from best friends to sisters.

MY VERY BEST FRIEND
IN THE WHOLE WIDE WORLD
Victoria Austen Moon

I recently spent a few days with my brother's family. Since I live several states away, I hadn't seen my niece and nephews for months, and it was a joy to discover how they'd grown, what they were learning in school, and all about their friendships.

"Who's your best friend?" I asked my four-year-old niece, Emily, who had just started pre-school. She wrinkled her brow in deep thought, then smiled.

"Rachel with short hair," she answered confidently. "And the other Rachel, the one with long hair. And Sarah. They're my best friends."

"But who's your one very best friend in the whole wide world?" I teased her.

She rolled her eyes at her seemingly slow-witted aunt. "They're all my best friends, silly!" she said, and jumped off my lap to play with her Barbie dolls.

That night, when I was putting Emily to bed, she asked me who my best friend was.

"Your mommy," I answered without hesitation.

"Why?" she questioned, and I smiled as I wondered how to answer such a big question.

Pam and I met when I was in eighth grade and she was in ninth. At first, I had a hard time understanding why this pretty, outgoing, popular blond girl wanted to pal around with a shy, skinny, unpopular brunette like me. Maybe it was our shared love of the Muppets, Rick Springfield, Swedish fish, and the Go-Gos. Maybe it was the way we could both spend an hour picking out fifty cents' worth of candy at the penny candy store down the street or sing the jingles from a hundred different television commercials.

As the years passed, Pam and I remained inseparable, despite attending different high schools and living ten miles apart. We were as comfortable doing each other's makeup as we were having our infamous free-for-all food fights. We spent the summers together at the beach, and she spent every weekend at my house. We called each other every afternoon, and we shared clothes, secrets, and crushes.

When she was sixteen, she confessed that she was in love—with my brother, Greg. He finally noticed her, too, and they began dating. When she turned eighteen they got engaged, and they married straight out of high school. It seemed perfect: my best friend was my sister-in-law. But we'd already started drifting apart.

Pam was rooted in the farmlands and church community where my brother served as a minister. I was a single, free-spirited artist and college student. Pam's letters to me were filled with her desire to have a baby, marriage, housework, and church potluck suppers; mine to her were filled with poetry, doomed love affairs, college classes, and tales of trying to write the great American novel in all-night diners. While she grew her hair out far past her shoulders and dressed in Laura Ashley prints and ballet flats, I cut my hair off to crew-cut length and stomped around in combat boots and ripped T-shirts. Though we no longer seemed to have anything in common, I still considered her to be my best friend. It was instinct, holding on to a piece of my past I didn't want to lose. More than that, I'd never found anyone to take her place in my heart.

In the Shade by Benjamin George Head. Image from Fine Art Photographic Library Ltd./Omell Gallery

Eventually my hair grew out, I became a freelance writer, and I fell in love with an architect. We were married in 1995. By then, Pam was a full-time, stay-at-home mom with two children and one on the way. Though our lives still couldn't have been more different, when it came time to choose my matron of honor, she was my first and only choice. She stood beside me like she always did, watching as I married the man I loved and laughing with me when her two-year-old son tore down the aisle during the ceremony to ask his aunt to come play outside with him.

In the years since, our lives have sometimes intersected, but more often they've detoured away from each other. We now live eleven hours apart; and, just when I left the corporate world to work at home, she started nursing school and working part-time outside her home. We still get together once or twice a year to grab a mug of tea and catch up. Within a minute or two, we usually pick up our conversation right where we last left it.

It is through these conversations that I've discovered it isn't our common interests that make our friendship so unique, it's our common history. It is seventeen years of laughter, tears, joy, and pain shared. Seeing one another at our best and worst has created an unconditional love and a bond that's grown deeper as we've moved from children to adults, from best friends to sisters.

Emily, I hope you find a friend who is as loyal, funny, smart, and kind as your mom—my very best friend in the whole wide world.

Gathering Poppies by Henry John Yeend King.
Image from Fine Art Photographic Library Ltd./Graham Gallery

Auld Lang Syne

Lyrics by Robert Burns

TRADITIONAL

Should auld ac- quain - tance be for - got, And

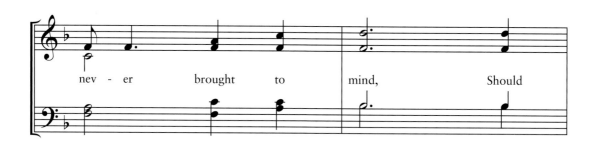

nev - er brought to mind, Should

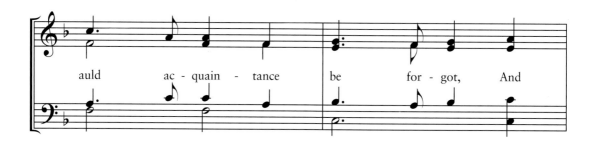

auld ac- quain - tance be for - got, And

days o' Lang Syne; For

Auld Lang Syne, my dear, For

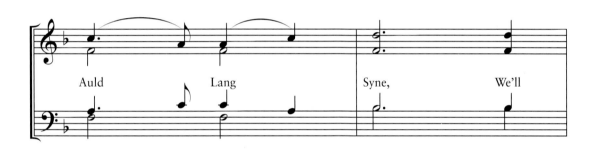

Auld Lang Syne, We'll

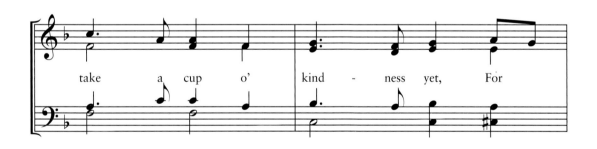

take a cup o' kind - ness yet, For

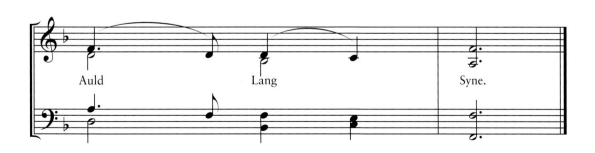

Auld Lang Syne.

A CELEBRATION OF FRIENDSHIP

My Old Friend

JAMES WHITCOMB RILEY

You're a manner all so mellow,

My Old Friend,

That it cheers and warms a fellow,

My Old Friend,

Just to meet and greet you and

Feel the pressure of a hand

That one may understand,

My Old Friend.

Though dimmed in youthful splendor,

My Old Friend,

Your smiles are still as tender,

My Old Friend,

And your eyes as true a blue

As your childhood ever knew,

And your laugh as merry too,

My Old Friend.

For though your hair is faded,

My Old Friend,

And your step a trifle jaded,

My Old Friend,

Old Time, with all his lures

in the trophies he secures,

Leaves young that heart of yours,

My Old Friend.

And so it is you cheer me,

My Old Friend,

For to know you still are near me,

My Old Friend,

Makes my hope of clearer light

And my faith of surer sight

And my soul a purer white,

My Old Friend.

Is there anything good to be said for the passage of time?
Here is one thing: it's the only way you get to be old friends.
There just isn't any shortcut to the long run.

—ELLEN GOODMAN

In the Garden by Wilhelm Menzler. Image from
Fine Art Photographic Library Ltd./
Courtesy of Anthony Mitchell, Nottingham

OLD FRIENDS, NEW FRIENDS

Pamela Kennedy

"Make new friends, but keep the old; one is silver, the other gold." This little verse learned in childhood holds much truth, and like a blossoming flower, it is a truth that unfolds gradually throughout our lives, exposing itself a bit at a time until it stands full-blown and beautiful before us.

What a joy and treasure old friends are; nuggets of gold that enrich our lives. Old friends, like old slippers, are easy to enjoy. They understand the peculiar bumps and wrinkles of our personalities and fit around them comfortably. Old friends never ask, "Now why did you do that or say that?" or "What did you mean?" They stood beside us as life buffeted and molded us, and they watched the process take place. They understand. Explanations aren't necessary and a glance can be a conversation with an old friend.

But sometimes they can push us, these old friends. Because they know our past, they often understand our potential and urge us to press on when we might long to quit. And that is precious too. Sometimes we need the vision of an old friend's love to become the best we can.

Old friends know the baggage we carry because often they were around when we first picked it up.

They remember the gawky, awkward girl buried inside the smart sophisticate; the longing romantic locked within the pragmatic executive. That knowledge gives us freedom to reveal our deepest thoughts and dreams. Old friends understand and accept us completely and help us know that what we are does not negate what we have become.

Old friends aren't afraid to share our sorrows. Their handclasp transmits love and caring more eloquently than words or flowery expressions of grief. They know the price we paid in time and energy and emotion, and when it all falls through, they stand beside us; and their support helps us maintain our balance.

Old friends are a treasure of inestimable value who give themselves to help enrich our lives. But what of new friends? They are faces whose names we've only learned; mysterious packages of personality we're just a bit afraid to open. These are treasures of a different kind: the sparkling, shining silver that brings to light new facets of ourselves.

For new friends challenge us to stretch and reach outside ourselves—and inside too. To try new things, acquire new skills, make new bonds with people who were strangers yesterday. They shake us from complacency and dare us to find within ourselves attributes we never knew we had.

New friends know nothing of our history except what we choose to reveal. They allow us the freedom to begin again, unencumbered by past failures and mistakes. Fresh as a silver morning, new friends permit us to embark on a new day at any point in life. They never saw the troubled teen, the unsure newlywed, the frazzled young mother. They see the now, the end result of all the yesterdays and the promise of tomorrow. New friends are the future. Their shining brightness calls us to go on without regret; to do something we've never done and be someone we've never been before.

Let us, then, not hide ourselves in the golden glow of an old friend's challenges. Let us learn to meld the two, enriching our lives immeasurably as the gold and silver intertwine, linking our lives in a precious chain of friendship.

A Tea Party in the Garden by Alfred Oliver. Image from Fine Art Photographic Library Ltd./Anthony Mitchell Paintings, Northampton

Friends

THOMAS CURTIS CLARK

If all the sorrows of this weary earth—
The pains and heartaches of humanity—
If all were gathered up and given me,
I still would have my share of wealth and worth
Who have you, Friend of Old, to be my cheer
Through life's uncertain fortunes, year by year.

Thank God for friends, who dearer grow
    as years increase;
Who, as possessions fail our hopes and hands,
Become the boon supreme, than gold and lands
More precious. Let all else, if must be, cease;
But, Lord of life, I pray on me bestow
The gift of friends, to share the way I go.

FRIENDLY FACES

Mark Twain

When we think of our friends—and call their faces out of the shadows, and their voices out of the echoes that faint along the corridors of memory, and do it without knowing why save that we love to do it—we content ourselves that that friendship is a reality, and not a fancy; that it is built upon a rock, and not upon the sands that dissolve away with the ebbing tides and carry their monuments with them.

Index